One of the more interesting and creative management books of the past few years, *The Springboard* reflects Denning's strong belief in stories as encapsulated knowledge and his own stories about the World Bank are strongly illustrative of his own passion and knowledge. Read it, and learn from it, and enjoy it!

—Larry Prusak, Co-author of *In Good Company: The Role of Social Capital in Organizations*

For me, reading *The Springboard* was just that, an amazing spring board for better understanding how to bring strategic change to organizations, how to communicate in ways that impact skeptical audiences and in general, how to rethink knowledge management from a customer perspective. It is also the best thing I have ever read on corporate communication.

—John Seely Brown, Chief Scientist, Xerox Corp, Co-author of *The Social Life of Information*

It is rare that a book works on so many levels. On one level, *The Springboard* tells the fascinating story of how the World Bank is harnessing knowledge for the biggest job of all: ending poverty around the world. On another level, Denning is disarmingly self-reflective about his own struggles to discover how to use stories to drive commitment and action in the Bank. And, finally, it works as a primer for anyone, anywhere, trying to build a picture of what's possible through stories. You won't forget the lessons learned, because the stories are so memorable. And that is part of the point, isn't it? What a good story.

—Jack Grayson, Chairman and Carla O'Dell, President, American Productivity & Quality Center (APQC)

Denning's book is a treasure. Perhaps it is the wonderful use of language, perhaps it is the insights offered, or perhaps it is his honesty as he tells the story. It is filled with wisdom that is easily embraced through the story he tells. I've never seen a book with so many quotable quotes per page. This book shows why real experience becomes more powerful as it is related through the surrounding story.

—Madelyn Blair, Consultant to Organizational Change Efforts, Pelerei, Inc.

*The Springboard* possesses the qualities of a classic, in that it captures the essence of very complex, dynamic, and fluid organizational situations and challenges in a very elegant, simple, effective, and even timeless manner. This book is an intellectual milestone on the road to organizational wisdom, a knowledge-era *Iliad* and *Odyssey* put together in a wonderful combination of the art and craft of organizational change management, a true management science epic.

—Professor Elias Carayannis, George Washington University

Denning's *The Springboard* is a dangerous tale, subtle at first reading, yet far reaching in its implications. If you want to learn how to change your company, your community, or even the world, this book will change you.

—Richard Stone, Author of *The Healing Power of Storytelling*

Hurray for this modern Aesop, who has provided his peers in management with a primer for the new millennium!

—James Donald Wilner, Architect

What strikes is the integrity of the story told. Astonishing and amazing honesty coupled with the drive to interest and progress.

—Professor Margaret Grieco,
Napier University, Edinburgh, Scotland

As a professional who uses storytelling in the business world to catalyze community, I have found *The Springboard* to be the manual I wish I had had ten years ago. Over and over again I appreciated his articulate description of the components and dynamics of good storytelling, and how to apply it in the world of business.

—Seth Weaver Kahan, Professional storyteller

Whether your interest is in knowledge management, organizational change, or leadership, be sure to read Stephen Denning's wonderful book about the key role of storytelling: his deeply personal account of his journey to transform the World Bank into a knowledge organization is everything he says a good "springboard" story should be— enjoyable, gripping, inspiring, eye-opening, and a springboard into new possibilities.

—Etienne Wenger, Author of *Communities of Practice*

This book should be in tool boxes of leaders and internal change consultants in every organization. Denning tells the inside story of an enormous change initiative at the World Bank.

—Mike Kaplan, Organizational facilitator

This is a wonderful book which is much larger than just a knowledge management, and it is even more than just a book about storytelling. It is a book about lightning insights, which mobilize and enliven a community, which, acting like strange attractors, bring a sense of meaning and purpose.

—Charles Savage, Author of *Fifth Generation Management*

Storytelling as a knowledge management technique is becoming very popular. This is a very readable and insightful book that should be of interest to practitioners everywhere.

—Ramon Barquin, Author of *Data Warehousing Fundamentals*

Never has there been so much concern with increasing organizational adaptability, with creating "learning organizations," with managing knowledge workers. A relevant body of literature is growing fast but is still thin, and seems thinnest in the how to do it dimension, making Denning's book particularly valuable. It is also beautifully written, at once literate and plainspoken.

—Visiting Professor Elliot Berg, University of Auvergne, France

A 106-year-old Chinese woman was asked the secret of her longevity. Her two word reply: "Welcome change." As Stephen Denning illustrates in his wonderful new book, *The Springboard*, most of us instead mightily resist change. As a project finance lawyer in the energy business, I deal with an international industry in the midst of profound change. *The Springboard* is a terrific tool to help lawyers and others communicate these changes to clients, lenders, regulators, and governments. It contains exciting and workable ideas that are conveyed in a refreshingly readable style. I particularly recommend it to lawyers and government executives.

—Lynn Hargis, Energy Lawyer and Arbitrator

This is a story of a reflective manager who listens to others and learns how to persuade others to listen to him; it is a story of how change really happens in large organizations. Denning's book is subtly and compellingly written and its messages are clear and strong. His story should resonate widely with all those who aspire to make a difference in organizations.

—Martine Haas, Harvard Business School

Denning's living portrait of the political, intellectual, and social challenges of moving knowledge management from an odd new idea to an active program offers valuable experiential wisdom to other managers who hope to win their organizations over to a new way of working.

—Don Cohen, Co-author of *In Good Company: The Role of Social Capital in Organizations*

On the surface, it all seems deceptively simple—just tell a story and the organization will change. Therein lies the paradox: on the surface, it is a simple story. Beneath the surface, though, is the story of Denning's quiet persistence in pursuing a strategy of shepherding, coaxing, and guiding others over whom he had no authority to go in the direction of that strategy.

—Lesley Shneier, Knowledge Management Specialist

Steve Denning's book is proof that he is a good storyteller. I kept wanting to read more and more. The power of story telling as a catalyst for change is clearly explained and he provides a guide for how the rest of us can follow his lead.

—Mitzi Wertheim, Center for Naval Analysis

*The Springboard* is profoundly important for everyone who is attempting to bring a community to life or induce a cultural shift into an organization.

—Michel Pommier, Knowledge Management Specialist

I had a hard time putting this book down. How often can one find a business tool that imparts true wisdom in its full context as only a story can do? This book does for the reader what the "springboard" story did for World Bank. Both of them enable the reader or the listener to see and become part of a higher purpose.

—Margo Corbett, Organizational change specialist

# The Springboard

How Storytelling Ignites Action in
Knowledge-Era Organizations

# The Springboard

## How Storytelling Ignites Action in Knowledge-Era Organizations

STEPHEN DENNING

BUTTERWORTH
HEINEMANN

Boston    Oxford    Auckland    Johannesburg    Melbourne    New Delhi

∞ Recognizing the importance of preserving what has been written, Butterworth–Heinemann prints its books on acid-free paper whenever possible.

GLOBAL ReLEAF Butterworth–Heinemann supports the efforts of American Forests and the ₂₀₀₀ Global ReLeaf program in its campaign for the betterment of trees, forests, and our environment.

This book was composed in Adobe Caslon font and designed by Diane DeMarco of Option C.

The views expressed in this book are the views of the author and do not necessarily represent the views of any other person or organization.

**Library of Congress Cataloging-in-Publication Data**
Denning, Stephen.
    The springboard: how storytelling ignites action in knowledge-era organizations/Stephen Denning.
        p. cm.
    Includes bibliographical references.
    ISBN 0-7506-7355-9 (pbk.: alk. paper)
    1. Communication in organizations. 2. Storytelling. I. Title.

HD30.3 .D46 2001
658.4'52—dc21

00-062093

**British Library Cataloguing-in-Publication Data**
A catalogue record for this book is available from the British Library.

The publisher offers special discounts on bulk orders of this book.
For information, please contact:
Manager of Special Sales
Butterworth–Heinemann
225 Wildwood Avenue
Woburn, MA 01801-2041
Tel: 781-904-2500
Fax: 781-904-2620

For information on all Butterworth–Heinemann publications available, contact our World Wide Web home page at: http://www.bh.com

10 9 8 7 6 5 4 3 2 1

Printed in the United States of America

# Table of Contents

# Introduction: Storytelling for Organizational Change

*If at first the idea is not absurd, then there is no hope for it.*

Albert Einstein

*My design here is not to teach the Method which everyone should fol-
low in order to promote the good conduct of his reason, but only to show
how I have endeavored to conduct my own.*

René Descartes, Discours de la Méthode[1]

**W**hy storytelling?

Nothing else worked.

Charts left listeners bemused.

Prose remained unread.

Dialogue was just too laborious and slow.

Time after time, when faced with the task of persuading a group of managers or front-line staff in a large organization to get enthusiastic about a major change, I found that storytelling was the only thing that worked.

This book is thus the story of how I stumbled upon the power of storytelling. I have to thank colleagues for prodding me onwards.

How do you get managements to understand a radical new idea? How do you transmit concepts, attitudes, and skills that are barely

---

[1] René Descartes, *Discourse on the Method and Meditations on First Philosophy*, edited by David Weissman, translated by Elizabeth S. Haldane and G.R.T. Ross. New Haven and London: Yale University Press, 1996, p. 4.

understood in the first place? How do you talk to the members of an organization and explain that what they have done for the past years, or even decades, has to be jettisoned? How do you instill positive new attitudes to changes that are complex, difficult, disruptive, strange, and counterintuitive? How do you get, not just acceptance, but enthusiasm and forward motion?

These pointed questions were put to me by colleagues facing fundamental shifts in their business environments, in organizations that were proving immovable. Where top managements didn't grasp the need for change, the consequences for the firm were potentially disastrous. Where top managements themselves were pushing change, "comply or say goodbye" was becoming the order of the day, with organizations going through painful periods of coercive persuasion, or starting with new populations of staff and managers who held different assumptions in the first place.[2] The unattractiveness and inefficiency of such practices were striking.

## ANOTHER WAY: STORYTELLING

This book is the story of how I chanced upon another way, that of catalyzing change through storytelling. I found that a certain sort of story enables change by providing direct access to the living part of the organization. It communicates complicated change ideas while generating momentum toward rapid implementation. It helps an organization reinvent itself.

Storytelling gets inside the minds of the individuals who collectively make up the organization and affects how they think, worry, wonder, agonize, and dream about themselves and in the process create—and re-create—their organization. Storytelling enables the individuals in an organization to see themselves and the organization in a

---

[2] Edgar H. Schein, "Empowerment, coercive persuasion and organizational learning: do they connect?" *The Learning Organization* (1999), Vol. 6, No. 4, pp. 163–172.

different light, and accordingly take decisions and change their behavior in accordance with these new perceptions, insights, and identities.

The attractions of narrative are obvious. Storytelling is natural and easy and entertaining and energizing. Stories help us understand complexity. Stories can enhance or change perceptions. Stories are easy to remember. Stories are inherently non-adversarial and non-hierarchical. They bypass normal defense mechanisms and engage our feelings. With all these strengths, I began looking into why the potential of storytelling had such little recognition.

I quickly found that I was living in an age when storytelling was suspect. Scientists derided it. Philosophers threatened to censor it. Logicians had difficulty in depicting it. Management theorists generally ignored it. And storytelling's bad press was not new. It had been disreputable for several millennia, ever since Plato identified poets and storytellers as dangerous fellows who put unreliable knowledge into the heads of children and hence would be subject to strict censorship in *The Republic*.3

The antagonism toward storytelling may have reached a peak in the twentieth century with the determined effort to reduce all knowledge to analytic propositions, and ultimately physics or mathematics. In the process, we discovered the limits of analytic thinking. We learned of Gödell's proof of the incompleteness of arithmetic, and began to absorb the implications of the indeterminacy of quantum physics and complexity theory, but many years of schooling had instilled in us a continuing itch for reductionist simplicity. This itch reflects what Freeman Dyson calls the Napoleonic approach, and leads to hierarchy, procedures, rules, and a distinctive form of myopia. It doesn't help us much in coping with a rapidly changing world, where innovation is the key to success.4

---

3 Plato, *The Republic*, Books 2–3. (Penguin Classics), translated by Desmond Lee. Viking Press, 1979.

4 Anthony Wensley, "The Value of Story Telling." *Knowledge and Process Management* (1998), Vol. 5, No. 1, pp. 1–2; Freeman Dyson, *Imagined Worlds (Jerusalem-Harvard Lectures)*, Harvard University Press, 1998, p. 52.

## THE TOLSTOYAN APPROACH

Innovation—what Dyson calls the creative chaos and freedom of the Tolstoyan approach[5]—swims in the richness and complexity of living. It breeds on the connections between things. As participants, we can grasp the interrelatedness of things in the world—and so are able to connect them in new ways—much more readily than when we are seeing them as an external observer through the window of rigid analytic propositions.

I found that the resistance to rethinking the role of storytelling was considerable. Academics suggested that even doing research on storytelling might drag the world back into the Dark Ages of myth and fable from which science had only recently extricated us. When I advocated storytelling, I often found myself at odds with those in authority—teachers, leaders, managers—who, ever since Plato, had been busy trying to hammer the square pegs of analytical thought into the round holes in our brains. The pain and wasted time of these efforts were enormous.

When I saw how easily round-edged stories could slide into our minds, I found myself wondering whether our brains might not be hard-wired to absorb stories. For purely pragmatic reasons, I ended up following what Plato, as one of the greatest storytellers of all time, actually practiced—and told stories.

The standard management manual, written in the rigid grip of theory, relies almost entirely on analytic thinking. Fix the systems. Re-engineer processes. Enhance quality. Streamline procedures. Reform and flatten the organizational structure. Analyze things in terms of grids and charts. Develop plans in which individuals are programmed

---

5 Dyson, 52ff. The Russian literary critic Mikhail Bakhtin detected Napoleonic tendencies even in Tolstoy, whom he saw as submerging different perspectives in one single authorial perspective. Bakhtin contrasted Tolstoy with Dostoevsky, whom he saw as allowing the voice of the narrator to coexist with those of the characters. In Dostoevsky, the voices intersect and interact in polyphonic dialogue: Mikhail Bakhtin, *Problems of Dostoevsky's Poetics* (translated by Caryl Emerson. Minneapolis, London: University of Minnesota Press, 1999), p. 56.

to operate like so many obedient computers. Hone our interpersonal mechanics and build skill inventories. Bring to our difficulties a fix-it attitude, as though our past errors can be easily corrected with straightforward explanations.

The cheerful optimism of this thinking sheds little light on why some organizations flourish and grow and are widely admired, and then suddenly collapse with the abruptness of a punctured balloon, or why some managements endure the most severe tribulations and difficulties, while others stumble at even a mild bump. The mechanistic analysis that we have applied to these problems has not always been of much help to us. It doesn't fit the complexity, the mess, the jumble, the clutter, the chaos, the confusion, the living core of modern organizations. And it rarely succeeds in persuading organizations to change.

This book is about understanding relationships through stories, from the point of view of a participant who is living, breathing, and acting in the world. It shows how storytelling is able to assist in mobilizing large numbers of managers and employees to understand complex and difficult changes. It tells how storytelling can enable a leap in understanding so that the audience intuitively grasps what the change involves and why it might be desirable, as well as pointing to how an organization or community might change.

## Storytelling Complements Abstract Analysis

Storytelling doesn't replace analytical thinking. It supplements it by enabling us to imagine new perspectives and new worlds, and is ideally suited to communicating change and stimulating innovation. Abstract analysis is easier to understand when seen through the lens of a well-chosen story and can of course be used to make explicit the implications of a story. This book does not recommend abandoning abstract thinking, nor does it suggest that we should give up the advances that have emerged through experimentation and science. I discuss here the discovery of the power of storytelling and the mechanisms by which it operates, thus remedying the neglect of story-telling, but not so as to jettison analytic thinking. I propose marrying the communicative and imaginative strengths of storytelling with the advantages of abstract and scientific analysis. Chapter 10 of this book examines the various options that are available to achieve a good marriage. Chapter 11 explores the difficulties that a cognitive scientist encounters in understanding the marriage. The final chapter discusses how the marriage of narrative and analysis itself evolves as a change idea becomes accepted by an organization.

## THE USE OF STORIES TO CHANGE THE WORLD

Despite the academic hostility to narrative, storytelling is pervasive in our lives. It has been at the heart of our communications since the beginning of the human race. Through stories, our values and principles have been passed from one generation to another. Stories provide continuity in our lives, conveying a sense of where we have come from, our history, and our heritage. Stories are immediate and unique. They celebrate how previous generations dealt with dilemmas in their lives. Storytelling brings people together in a common perspective, and stretches everyone's capacity to empathize with others and share experience. In this way stories have been used to strengthen culture.[6] This book, however, is not so much about using stories to preserve organizations: it's about using stories to change them.

It's about a particular kind of story, which I will christen here the *springboard story*. By a springboard story, I mean a story that enables a leap in understanding by the audience so as to grasp how an organization or community or complex system may change.

---

[6] Karl E. Weick and Larry D. Browning, "Argument and Narration in Organizational Communication," *Yearly Review of Management of the Journal of Management,* edited by J.G. Hund and J.D. Blair (1986), Vol. 12, No. 2, pp. 243–259. See also Richard Stone, *The Healing Art of Storytelling: A Sacred Journey of Personal Discovery.* New York: Hyperion, 1996.

A springboard story has an impact not so much through transferring large amounts of information, as through catalyzing understanding. It can enable listeners to visualize from a story in one context what is involved in a large-scale transformation in an analogous context. It can enable them to grasp the idea as a whole not only very simply and quickly, but also in a nonthreatening way. In effect, it invites them to see analogies from their own backgrounds, their own contexts, their own fields of expertise.

## THE CHARACTERISTICS OF SPRINGBOARD STORIES

I found that not all stories had the springboard effect. In this book, I describe why springboard stories worked well with particular audiences—and why they didn't with others—and the principles that can help us choose stories that will work with audiences to achieve a particular effect.

The stories that were successful for me all had certain characteristics. They were stories that were told from the perspective of a single protagonist who was in a predicament that was prototypical of the organization's business. The predicament of the explicit story was familiar to the particular audience, and indeed, it was the very predicament that the change proposal was meant to solve. The story had a degree of strangeness or incongruity for the listeners, so that it captured their attention and stimulated their imaginations. Yet at the same time, the story was plausible, even eerily familiar, almost like a premonition of what the future was going to be like. I took steps to ensure that story embodied the change proposal to the fullest extent possible, using real examples from within the organization, and sometimes extrapolating into the future to complete the picture. The stories were told as simply and as briefly as possible. Speed and conciseness of style were keys, because as an instigator of change, I was less interested in conveying the details of what exactly happened in the explicit story than I was in sparking new stories in the minds of the listeners, which they would invent in the context of their own environments. For the same reason, the stories all had "happy endings": this seemed to make it easy for the listeners to make the imaginative leap from the explicit story that I was telling, to the implicit story that I was trying to elicit in their minds. Chapters 8–10 are explicitly focused on crafting, building, and performing springboard stories.[7]

## CLOSING THE KNOWING–DOING GAP THROUGH STORYTELLING

Just think if we were able to operate in that way, and get those kinds of benefits at that kind of speed! Wouldn't that be exciting? What kind of organization could we become? If the listeners are stimulated to think actively about the implications, they can understand what it will be like to be doing things in a different way. When a springboard story does its job, the listeners' minds race ahead, to imagine the further implications of elaborating the same idea in other contexts, more intimately known to the listeners. In this way, through extrapolation from the narrative, the re-creation of the change idea can be successfully brought to birth, with the concept of it planted in listeners' minds, not as a vague, abstract, inert thing, but an idea that is pulsing, kicking, breathing, exciting—and alive.

Often the changes that need to be implemented in large organizations are complicated and have many dimensions and facets. Not all of them are fully understood when the management embarks on the change process. Resistance is inevitable when a bold new change idea emerges. The dilemma for managements in such situations is how to turn resistance into enthusiasm when even they only partially understand the idea themselves. Often the attempt to explain the idea can kill enthusiasm before it even begins implementation. The book shows how stories can avoid this dilemma by having the listeners themselves fill in the blanks as the change process proceeds.

---

[7] See also Appendixes 1–5.

## THE CONTEXT OF THIS BOOK: KNOWLEDGE MANAGEMENT

This book tells the story that storytelling played in the process of sparking organizational change. It's not primarily about the particular change idea—which happens to be knowledge management—or the particular organization in which it was adopted—which happens to be the World Bank. The focus here is on one particular aspect of the process by which the change idea was introduced. In focusing on this facet of the transformation, I am conscious of having done scant justice to the broader story of what was going on in the organization, of which I was only a part. Also, many of the issues and problems of implementing knowledge management will go unexplored.

## DO STORIES ALWAYS WORK?

Storytelling is not a panacea for eliciting change in organizations. It can only be as good as the underlying idea being conveyed. If that idea is bad, storytelling may well reveal its inadequacy. But even when the underlying idea is good, there are times when storytelling is ineffective. The book describes occasions when the listeners simply didn't grasp the concept at all. There were people, for instance, who listened to my stories, and instead of comprehending the underlying change idea, pressed me with questions for more detail. When this happened, I knew that we were getting into a discussion of the explicit story. These were interesting issues, but they also indicated that the story had failed to elicit the implicit story, and so spring the listener to a new level of understanding of the possibilities of knowledge sharing and of the organizational change being envisaged.

## THE IMPACT OF STORYTELLING

The book shows how when a story works well with its audience, it embeds a way of looking at the world in the listeners' minds, so as to induce in their thinking a mental geography of the organization and the world with new planes of order and opportunity. Each time we enter the word-woven magic of a story, our lives are enlarged, as we give ourselves to another mode of knowing. In the process, an understanding of the potential of the change idea can erupt into the collective consciousness, producing a sudden coalescence of vision in the minds of listeners. The provenance of these thoughts—in this instance, the story—is not even very important. What matters is the fact that they happen and their inherent quality and where they are headed next. The spark that starts the fire is less significant than the conflagration that then takes place.

## THE FORCE OF ORAL STORYTELLING

In this book, I describe the success that I had with telling stories face-to-face with listeners in a live performance, along with the very limited success that I experienced in using stories in print or video. Others may have more success with print and video than I had. I am simply reporting here what I encountered. In effect, my experience was that *storytelling*, more than *stories per se*, was having the impact. The look of the eye, the intonation of the voice, the way the body was held, the import of a subtle pause, and my own response to the audience's responses—all these aspects seemed to make an immense contribution to the meaning of a story for my audiences. I devote a chapter of this book to discuss how to use the performance of storytelling for maximum effect.[8] It may seem paradoxical that I, who spent much of my professional life exploiting and promoting the strengths of electronic technology, now found myself relying on the ancient art of face-to-face storytelling—but that's what happened. Oral storytelling enabled me to use the uniquely focused dynamics of direct address, knitting question to answer and living voice to living reception.[9]

---

[8] Chapter 9. See also Appendixes 2 and 3.

[9] George Steiner, *Martin Heidegger*. Chicago: University of Chicago Press, 1989, p. xiv.

Readers will need to keep the oral dimension of storytelling in mind as they read this book, since some of the stories told in print in this book, when read in the cold white light of the printed page, may seem so brief and undramatic and bland that it may not be easy to see how they could have had the impact that they had. The options for me as author were either to report the stories verbatim as they were told, or to adjust and embellish the stories with literary techniques to make them more suitable for written transmission. I have opted for the former approach, so as to make transparent the mechanics of story-telling. Thus, the reader will need to remember when reading the stories that they were told in person, and read them as one reads a text of a theatrical performance, adding—in their imagination—the sound of the storyteller's voice and the presentation setting.

## A Way of Accelerating Change

This book describes my experiences in using stories to help people and organizations that I knew to effect change. I put this history on the laboratory table, so to speak, so that others might examine it, dissect it, learn from it, and, in due course, conduct their own experiments from which a more comprehensive and consistent body of knowledge might emerge.

# PART I

# *Practice*

# ONE

# Stumbling upon the Springboard Story

*But regarding this Treatise as simply a history, or, if you prefer it, as a fable, in which, among certain things which may be imitated, there are possibly others also which it would not be right to follow, I hope that it will be of use to some without being harmful to any, and that all will thank me for my frankness.*

René Descartes, *Discours de la Méthode*[1]

Around noon, the dry, odorless, conditioned air in the fifth floor of the office building where I work succumbs to a faint whiff of French fries and Chinese food that makes its way up the elevator shaft from the cafeteria on the ground floor, or from the communal microwave ovens in which penny-pinching assistants heat meals hand-carried from tiny apartments in the outlying suburbs of Washington, D.C., or from the sandwiches that some of us purchase and bring to our desks to munch in front of multicolored computer screens. Often we eat alone, oblivious to any kind of social nicety, or the weather outside, totally immersed in our work, as if eager not to lose a moment in our efforts to advance the cause of poverty alleviation in the poorest coun-

---

[1] René *Descartes, Discourse on the Method and Meditations on First Philosophy*, edited by David Weissman, translated by Elizabeth S. Haldane and G.R.T. Ross. New Haven and London: Yale University Press, 1996, p. 5.

3

tries of the world, which is the daunting mission of the international organization where we work.

It is March 1996. Today, I am sharing a brown-bag lunch around the conference table in my office with a younger colleague. He is fair, fresh-faced, and engagingly idealistic. An economist in the health and education sectors, he has worked with me in various parts of the organization in the past. I am relieved to see that his sudden and recent ascension to be an adviser to one of the organization's top managers has endowed him with none of the hauteur and self-importance that sometimes come with these transitions. He has the same self-deprecating sense of humor that attracted me to him in the first place. He sees himself as an anomaly in the exalted echelons of top management, where he is treated gently as a sounding board for the men and women in the trenches. He is learning what it is to work in those sublime heights. Although he doesn't seem to regret my advice to take the position for a limited time, he is keen to get back to working directly with clients on the front lines. He has generally proved receptive to new ideas. When I ask him to come to share some sandwiches in my office, he accepts at once and is immediately eager to hear what I have to say.

⤳

A month prior to this lunch, I had been asked by the management to look into the issue of information in our organization. As a manager in operations in the organization for several decades, I had not been especially happy to get this request, since my professional life and enjoyment lay in face-to-face dealings with clients, traveling to remote countries around the globe, seeing for myself what was happening on the spot, and solving problems with everyone from heads of state to villagers and children. At the time, I had no desire to leave this kind of life. This was what I liked doing and what I thought I knew how to do. Why should I leave this exciting world and look into the unglamorous issue of information, a field of expertise in which I was no more than an enthusiastic amateur? The answer wasn't obvious to me or anyone else. At the time, information was considered a low-status and low-priority occupation in the organization. The shift from operations to information was universally regarded as a move to an organizational backwater. It caused everyone to wonder why I would consider it, let alone agree.

And yet I was not exactly angry. I was even a little intrigued with the idea of looking full-time into the issue of information. As an early advocate of personal computing who had felt the exhilaration and liberation that it offered, I had some inkling of the potential. Yet the institutional issues that it generated were immense. The costs were high and rising, and the benefits not yet evident. Many of the basics were not in place: every question on even the simplest issue, such as how many clients we had, or how much money we had spent on anything, had multiple answers. There was no strategic vision of the role of information, which existed in silos and was inaccessible across the organization. Periodic efforts at cleanup were fragmented and generally short-lived. Despite the high costs of maintaining information, there seemed to be little benefit from our information systems for external clients and partners in running the organization's business.

Which business *were* we in? On this central issue, even among the top management, there was little consensus. Traditionally, our organization had been conceived as a *financial* organization, transferring money through loans for development projects in the poorest countries of the world—getting kids into school in Bolivia, sparking rural development in Uganda or health development in Kenya, igniting private sector growth in Thailand, remedying gender disparities in Zambia, or protecting the environment in Brazil. Over time, however, the organization had acquired additional functions, as a *coordinator* of transactions with the countries in which the organization operated, as a catalyst or promoter of additional financial sources and transactions in those countries, and as a *knowledge broker*, through the transfer of information and know-how to people and organizations on how to get results in those countries. It was this last function, that of knowledge broker, that had been steadily growing in practical importance over the years. Initially it had occurred as a natural by-product of financing development projects, but there were increasing opportunities to transfer this know-how independently of any financial transaction, and indeed the advent of the World Wide Web dramatically expanded those possibilities. Clients were becoming more demanding in terms of the quality of the advice that the organization provided. They were increasingly dissatisfied with merely receiving the expertise of the individuals who happened to have been assigned to handle their affairs. Instead, they were beginning to insist on getting the best expertise from around the globe that the entire organization could provide, and if we couldn't offer that, they would go elsewhere to find it. It was striking that the only aspect of our organization's business that was significantly supported by the huge investment in information systems was the *financial transfer* business. The *coordinator, catalyst*, and *knowledge broker* functions were essentially being conducted on a craftlike basis, with one-on-one transactions handled in person or on paper. Despite an immense wealth of professional expertise in the staff of the organization, there were, apart from a couple of isolated pilot efforts, no consistent and systematic actions to establish and maintain access to the organization's knowledge or to extend its potential reach. The potential partners of those various businesses—coordinator, catalyst, and knowledge broker—were so numerous that the craft mode of operation was increasingly incapable of coping. Unless a new mode of operation could be invented, these businesses were at risk of unraveling.

Even in the financial business, where systems already existed, there were immense information inefficiencies. The simplest issue, such as disbursing funds for overseas projects, entailed a large-scale paper chase. One might imagine that in an era of electronic technology and ATM machines, the question of disbursing the money under a loan from a large modern organization would occur in a matter of minutes. In our organization, the task was far more arduous and the normal lead time was in weeks or even months. Thus, even after loans were agreed, the borrower would deliver a complicated paper-based withdrawal application to the field office of our organization in the place where the disbursement had occurred. The field office would log in the application, which would enter a pile of disbursement applications. The collection of applications would in due course be placed in the pouch and flown to New York, where it would be sorted and flown to Washington, D.C. From here, it would find its way through the mail room to the disbursement department and enter a queue of paper applications awaiting attention from the staff. In due course, the disbursement application would be logged in again, enter a new queue, and eventually be processed, so that an instruction would be sent to the cashier's department to issue a check, and thus eventually—some two to four weeks after the borrower submitted the paper application, if there was not some other snafu—the payment would actually be made. Everyone was doing his or her job expeditiously and diligently. No single individual was causing the delay. It was the overall system that had to be dismantled, so that funds could be disbursed in minutes, not weeks or sometimes months.

The problems of our organization in managing information thus were obvious. But what made the prospect of reform so unpromising was that these problems had all been repeatedly documented. In 1988, the internal audit department had written a report pointing out the need for policies, procedures, and controls in the management of information. In 1989, the audit department had produced another report to the effect that enhanced information management was essential for the organization to maintain its competitive edge. In 1993, a comprehensive study concluded that the information systems in place were not responsive to the organization's business needs. In 1995, three separate reports had reached the same conclusion. All these reports had three features in common. One was that they had all correctly identified the huge unresolved problems that the organization was facing in managing its information systems. Secondly, they all refrained from recommending comprehensive solutions to those problems. Apparently, immense bureaucratic inertia and territorial defensiveness had set in whenever anyone had dared suggest remedying a

setup that was untenable. Thirdly, the outcome in each case was identical. It simply led to yet another study.

Fixing the information systems would thus not only be
immensely difficult. It was, as everyone was quick to tell me, utterly
unrealistic.

Yet something else—less obvious—was also bothering me. Even
if the existing information systems did get fixed, and the reforms were
a glorious success, the organization would not be very different. It
would move more quickly. After some initial investment, it would cost
somewhat less to run. Clients might find it somewhat easier to deal
with. But it would still be in the same business. It would still be at risk
of competition from a new breed of financial organization in the private sector that was increasingly providing finance to the less-devel-
oped countries. It would not be adding much more value to its clients,
who would remain the somewhat limited circle of beneficiaries of its
financial transactions. The potentially broader audience for the treasure house of expertise that our professionals possessed would not be
helped even by a fully successful reform of the existing information
systems.

Thus, my intuition told me I had been given the wrong riddle.
Information was yesterday's issue. Our real opportunity was in
knowledge.

Knowledge offered a lot. If we could rapidly share good practice
and make know-how widely accessible, then a more agile and more
broadly useful organization might emerge. The idea of sharing
knowledge was not new, and in fact was spreading across many for-
ward-looking organizations under the paradoxical labels of "knowledge management," "intellectual asset management," or "the learning
organization."

So I found myself setting aside the mandate that management
had proposed—to look into the issue of information—and instead,
putting together a coalition of colleagues who understood how valuable the whole approach of sharing know-how and expertise could be
and who could help transform the organization's strategy.

It was an exciting but difficult time for me. I spent my days prowling the organization's corridors and cafeteria, buttonholing anyone I could find, and dragging them to my office if they would come—or talking to them on the spot if they wouldn't—to tell them about the idea of knowledge sharing that had taken hold of me. My spirits were not a little depressed, as I was finding it difficult to get anyone to listen. Most of the people couldn't or wouldn't seem to understand an idea that seemed to me so obvious and logical and self-evident. To them, the notion was strange and incomprehensible and outlandish, almost contrary to common sense, as if coming from another planet. I was heavy with pessimism that the message would ever get across. In my desperation, I was improvising, trying things out, sensing the reactions of single individuals, getting their suggestions, struggling to understand their puzzlement, jettisoning anything that didn't fully connect, and accentuating any ideas that seemed to strike a chord and resonate.

⌒

On this day in March 1996, as I sit with my colleague eating ham sandwiches and talking and swapping stories of our respective experiences, and discussing the idea of knowledge sharing, he tells me about something that has happened to him recently. He has been traveling in Africa—in Zambia, a country about the size of France but with only a fifth of the population and very low incomes—where he is working on a investment project aimed at improving health services to families, particularly mothers and children, and he had come across a health worker in Kamana, a small town some 600 kilometers from the capital of the county, Lusaka. The health worker was trying to find the solution to a problem in treating malaria.

I have never been to Kamana, but I have been to Zambia several times, and know that it is one of the least developed countries in the world. At independence in 1964, it was a prosperous copper-producing economy, but mismanagement of economic policy over several decades has left the country with a huge debt, run-down infrastructure, and collapsing health facilities and schools. Government services are short of resources to an extent that is practically unimaginable in developed countries. All services have difficulties in getting enough funds to make anything happen. Our organization is involved in helping the Zambians redress the legacy of economic mismanagement in various sectors, including health. I know how desperate it is to be a health worker in an out-of-the-way place like Kamana with such limited resources. In the heat and the dust and the flies, there is often no running water, no reliable electricity, few telephones, unpaved roads, no drugs, no bandages, no equipment, and no reliable transport. In such places, the living and working conditions are so distressingly difficult that it is almost a miracle if any health services get delivered at all. Access to real expertise is more than an expensive luxury, almost an impossible dream.

My colleague tells me about a health worker in Kamana, who in June 1995 logged on to the Center for Disease Control Web site and got the answer to a question on how to treat malaria. He thinks that it's a neat illustration of how the idea of knowledge sharing across organizations is already working. At least one person in one of the least developed countries of the world has found something useful on the Web. This is, remember, early 1996, and the Web has not attained the widespread recognition as a potential purveyor of useful information that it will enjoy only a year or so later. The example shows that medical expertise existing on a Web site in Atlanta can lead to low-cost sharing of know-how with a health worker in a rural area on the other side of the globe—even in an out-of-the-way place like Kamana, with such limited resources, with so few educated people, with so little in the way of communications facilities. I am beginning to think: if it can work there, then why can't it work on a very large scale—not just in health, but in all fields of expertise, across Zambia, across Africa, across the entire planet?

The glimmerings of the implications are there, but the conversation moves on, and we part without any recognition on my part that anything particularly magical has happened. The Zambia story is a fascinating anecdote, but neither of us see much significance beyond this. We are just a couple of guys having sandwiches together, exchanging stories, talking of everything and nothing, drawing on the vast organizational stream of consciousness, with the flow of the significant and trivial, the flotsam and jetsam of organizational life. The Zambia story is simply another twig floating by, a single analogy in a different organization of the general hypothesis of organizational change that I am putting forward.

But I do realize that the example can be incorporated into my arsenal of arguments. Up to this time, I've been having little success in getting anyone to accept that our organization has anything other than a financial future that is an extrapolation of the present. The word *bank* is in the very name of our organization. "We're a bank, right?" the managers say with a tone of finality, as if that settles the matter. A glance at the balance sheet confirms that we do indeed lend a lot of money—several tens of billions of dollars every year. Our financial assets add up to more than $100 billion. To simple individuals, such masses of money are not only unimaginable: they are hard to argue with. Even those childhood exercises intended to explain the meaning of large numbers by pointing to analogies—such as by starting from the idea that a cup of coffee costs about a dollar and then thinking of twenty billion coffee cups that can be laid in a row that is more than enough to stretch to the moon and back—doesn't really seem to make either the number or the sum of money any more manageable or understandable. Such hugeness only tends to dwarf us all, confirm our insignificance as individuals, and reinforce our seeming inability to influence such size. The very bigness of the numbers leads on to an irresistible and relentless conclusion that it scarcely matters what we as individuals might think. The money has its own dynamic.

Once such seemingly unbelievable sums of money exist, and are under our jurisdiction, obvious consequences follow. Projects supported by loans have to be supervised. Existing loans have to be repaid. New loans have to be made; otherwise old borrowers will be caught short of funds. Lending has a cycle of identification, preparation, appraisal, supervision, and evaluation that leads inevitably to yet more loans. Lending targets have to be met. The machinelike reliability of the cycle is as relentless and self-evident to the managers and staff of our organization as the revolutions of the planets around the sun. The economies of entire countries could crumble if the lending machine is permitted to falter. Yes, giving advice to our clients on the side is conceivable, perhaps even desirable, but only as a minor by-line: it can hardly be considered on the same level of importance as lending. Lending is what makes our organization a major world player. Even if we want to get off this perpetual motion machine, it simply isn't possible. Lending not only pays everyone's salary: it is also one of the pillars of the international financial system. To people thinking in this mode, knowledge doesn't offer a genuine option, but rather risks causing a distraction from the organization's *raison d'être*, of disrupting the financial lifeline. The suggestion that we might have anything other than a financial destiny is akin to attacking something hallowed, undermining the fundament, or tampering with the very fabric of our reality. It is as if merely thinking of the possibility of an alternative carries with it an intrinsic risk of instability, a vision whose very articulation will put in peril the stately grandeur of the status quo. The interlocking chain-mail logic of the underlying assumptions leads irresistibly to the mindset that the organization will be, and should be, committed to lending forever. So it has been. So it will always be. In this world, merely rational arguments about the way the world is changing and why knowledge will turn out to be more important than money sound flat and vacuous.

I can see the pained and questioning looks in my colleagues' eyes when I make the case for change. Their very faces tell me that they are not unhappy with the way things are. Their raised eyebrows ask: what has driven me to pose such questions? It's as if the mere suggestion of thinking about a different future for the organization is enough to bruise them. They have already given so much of their lives to the organization as it is that they relate to it more than anything else on earth. They know that it is flawed, but within the embrace of its imperfect bosom, they feel safe, satisfied, reconciled. The thought that it may change is by itself almost enough to open a wound. As I feel their hurt, it doesn't help that I become more animated and impassioned in making my case. It only heightens the sense that I am attacking in some fashion their personal adequacy and character, since in their own eyes, their very identities are enmeshed with their sense of the organization. I assure them this is not my intent, but I can see that the damage has already been done. They are eyeing the exit and looking for a way to escape.

In this situation, I am desperate for anything that can attract sympathetic attention. The Zambia story seems to offer a possibility, albeit tenuous. It shows that the idea of sharing know-how is not totally theoretical, not completely abstract and hypothetical. In effect, here it is, already operating in a different organization with direct benefits in Zambia, one of the least developed countries in the world. It has proved its worth in a real-life situation. Sharing expertise across the Web has actually happened. It is embryonic corroboration of the idea that I am promoting. I also recognize that by way of evidence it could hardly be more slender.

Nevertheless, anything is better than nothing. And so I decide to prepare a slide on the Zambia story and weave it into the presentations that I am making on the subject of sharing know-how.

⌒

In the weeks that follow my brown-bag lunch in March 1996, I use the anecdote of the Zambia health worker in my presentation to explain what knowledge sharing is about. From these presentations, it becomes apparent to me that the Zambia story is unexpectedly effective in communicating the idea of knowledge management. It steadily grows in importance in my presentations so that it becomes a kind of pivot point in my pitch for organizational change.

"What will the future be like?" I say in my presentations. "My sense is that it will be very much like today. Let me show you why from something that happened recently in Zambia. . . ."

I notice that when I use the Zambia story in this way, people are able to understand the idea of knowledge sharing. They seem to get the idea. When I use the story, their questions to me after the presentation show that they are beginning to grasp the complex and subtle set of changes that will be needed if the organization is to make a whole-hearted commitment to the systematic sharing of its expertise. With the Zambia story, something is beginning to click.

When I don't use the Zambia story, I find that the conversation often ends up in a tangle of debates about various aspects of the feasibility of the change idea. When I get into these debates, I try telling the Zambia story, but I find that it is much less effective in extinguishing a fire than in getting one started. Told as an *ex post* explanation, the Zambia story isn't considered as a way of understanding the idea from the inside, but rather as a sliver of evidence that has to be weighed in the scales, along with other contrary pieces of evidence. Viewed in such a way, the Zambia story adds practically nothing. People correctly question whether a single illustration of one person in one country could possibly show the feasibility of a whole approach on a global basis. They start to look at the particular features of the health scene in Zambia that might have caused such an aberration. "Was this particular health worker unusual in terms of training or expertise? What was idiosyncratic about the organizational environment? And how many cases are there like the Zambia health worker?" When such questions are posed, I have to confess that the health worker, to my knowledge, is unique: I have no other examples to hand, and hence the evidentiary value of a single instance is not by itself significant.

By contrast, when I use the story as a way of explaining the idea at the outset, I find that I don't get this kind of question. Listeners don't raise an issue with the Zambia story itself, and instead the discussion moves on to a positive search for ways in which an analogous approach can be implemented in our organization, in the kinds of work we do, the clients we deal with, the countries we work in, and the potential costs, risks, and benefits. When it is used as part of the initial presentation, the Zambia story seems to elevate the understanding of the group to a higher level. The discussion, instead of getting bogged down in *whether* to share knowledge, shifts to *how* to implement it.

◦⌇◦

As a result of these presentations, more and more staff at varying levels in our organization start hearing about the idea of knowledge sharing through the Zambia story. As these efforts to get the change idea accepted evolve, the Zambia story is becoming so central to my whole argument that I become worried that so much weight is resting on it. I need to check it out. I go back to my younger colleague and put the questions to him directly.

"It's a great story, but are we sure that it's true? Did it really happen that way? Could it be corroborated?"

Our organization's business is international development and the managers I am talking to have traveled in countries like Zambia. They have been in places like Kamana, six hundred kilometers from the capital, where the roads aren't paved, the water is not always drinkable, the power supply is variable, and communications not generally dependable.

Is it really possible that the health worker would have access to the Internet in such a place?

I am assured that it is not only possible but true: the health services project on which he was working helped finance a computer to enable communications internally within Zambia, and as a spin-off, access to the World Wide Web has also been provided. He has seen it himself. So it is plausible to have a World Wide Web connection.

I am somewhat reassured. And yet I am still nervous, but short of going to Zambia, actually meeting the health worker, and seeing the computer in use, there is not a great deal more that I can do to satisfy myself that the Zambia end of the story is accurate: if the question ever arises, my colleague says that he will be ready to verify it.

So much for the Zambian end, but what about Atlanta? I get the URL address of the Web site of the Centers for Disease Control and pay an electronic visit. Sure enough, it is packed with information on diagnosing and treating various diseases, including malaria. It is not a flashy Web site with a lot of glitz and whiz-bang graphics. Instead, it is sober with black print on white background in a quiet typewriter font. The experience of reading the material there is like viewing a printed manuscript. No one would ever say that it was entertaining, but the substance is there. I can imagine a health worker in Zambia getting access to it, and, if she knew what to look for, finding it a treasure trove of useful know-how. So someone in Kamana could well have found the answer to a problem confronting the health services in that area, six hundred miles from the Zambian capital, on the other side of the planet.

∽

The Zambia story is thus plausible, but what it doesn't answer is: how will knowledge sharing work in *our* organization? A stray hit on the CDC Web site is one thing. But what does it mean for us? How will we get organized so that we can share our expertise like CDC?

The Zambia story whets the imagination, but doesn't satisfy the appetite. How will the idea work in practice? What will it mean for the average task team, the people who do the work of our organization? How will it affect their working lives? I can see that the Zambia story poses the question, but doesn't provide the full answer.

As I try to think through the case for the change, I am also painfully aware of just how difficult it will be to implement the idea in practice.

∽

A year earlier, we had already had our first stab at knowledge management in the Africa section where I was working. Although in prospect, it had seemed so obvious and logical, nothing worked out as we had expected. In March 1995, it had been decided to establish a best practice system. It was to be a computerized database containing whatever our best professional staff knew about getting results on the ground in the fields of expertise where we were active. In the coming months, we would visit other organizations, such as the Big Six international consulting firms that had already established best practice systems. By July of that year, we would instruct our staff to compile what they considered to be their best practices. By September, we would open for business, and by the end of the year, we would have widespread use of the system.

In implementation, everything had turned out very differently. When we took our staff to look at the Big Six that had already established best practice systems, they told us bluntly: "This will never work for us." We inquired why not, and were told: "It doesn't fit our business." When we ignored this advice, and instructed our experts to get on with the job of compiling best practice, we could find very little compliance. When we asked why not, we got no coherent reply. We eventually figured out that the experts didn't know what best practice was, because they had not been able to agree among themselves. Every expert had a different idea of what was best. When we had pursued the issue and asked why the experts in the Africa section didn't consult the experts in the central part of our organization with so-called global expertise, we were told: "We don't agree with them, and they don't even agree among themselves. And besides, only one out of many central units has anything like a practice manager." When we suggested to our experts that it might be a good idea anyway to spend the time to agree among themselves what best practice really was, so that our clients might get the best advice that we could provide, the experts replied: "That's not our job. Our job is to meet with our clients and deal with their needs, not sit in an office in headquarters and assemble best practice manuals." The most frustrating aspect of the whole sequence had been that in the few areas where some experts did take any notice of our instructions to assemble a best practice system, the amount of material that was assembled quickly became so large and unwieldy that anyone who attempted to use it found it too cumbersome to find out what they wanted.

~

Thus, as I look back to these recent experiences, I can see that the idea of launching a system for sharing best practice and expertise, an idea that seemed so obvious and logical in foresight, quickly evolved into a significant problem.

Worse, as I look forward and try to imagine the future, I find that I cannot visualize precisely what the brave new world of knowledge sharing will be like. I don't have the capacity to imagine all of the transpositions that will be necessary to execute the change idea. I have a fuzzy, inchoate notion that it must be possible to organize the know-how and make it accessible to task teams in an easy, seamless fashion. I can visualize the big picture, but I lack the inventiveness to put flesh on the skeleton. There are too many variables. My imagination is inadequate.

Then a serendipitous visit to a computer software firm in the technology corridor at Tyson's Corner, Virginia, comes to the rescue. In advance of the visit, all I know is that the firm is doing "some interesting things." On this basis, on a bright sunny morning in the spring of 1996, two colleagues and I drive out to a modern office building in Tyson's Corner in suburban Washington, and we meet with several executives in an octagonal room with numerous desktop computers. We are offered some sandwiches on plastic plates for lunch, before being shown some work that they have going on.

There are several facets to the presentation. The firm is doing impressive things with computer networks that connect personal computers together. The firm is intimately involved in business process re-engineering, which is currently subject to criticism in the press for not having delivered on its promises. And they are developing the computer equivalent of a desktop for their professionals involved in business process re-engineering.

It is this third idea that I find exciting. The computerized desktop screen has buttons around the edges, so that at each stage of a project for business process re-engineering, the team working on the project can click on the buttons and get the best manuals and methodologies that the organization has been able to develop. In this way, the various teams can adopt a common approach, and so avoid making mistakes that have been made before. The tool is under construction and the difficulties of implementation are very evident, and yet the germ of an exciting idea is present: the analogy of the desktop, a place where professionals do their work, where they have access to everything they need to do the job—all the references, all the methodologies—all assembled around the edges of the electronic desktop, visible and easily within reach.

Not only that, the requests are context-sensitive. In other words, pressing the button doesn't give you everything that the firm has managed to collect. Instead, it gives the professional just the relevant pieces of expertise for that particular stage of the business process re-engineering. Instead of drinking from a fire hose, one receives a manageable, digestible helping—just enough and just in time. It is the germ of an idea as to what providing access to knowledge for task teams might be like.

On the way driving back from Virginia, my mind is racing ahead to my next presentation. Suppose we get ourselves organized? Suppose we do the same thing and develop a desktop with all of the relevant information and best practice that will enable a professional to get the job done. Suppose we have our data properly arrayed. What will a typical task team need? What will they want to have on the edges of their desktop? It isn't difficult to predict. It includes such things as good practices, a bibliography, policies and guidelines, most frequently asked questions and mistakes, country information, data and statistics, the text of previous work that has been done in the field, the identity of the experts in the subject, and analytical tools. But the key insight provided by the visit is that the professionals do not merely need access to large archives of such items: they need a selection of those elements that are relevant to the task at hand.

Thus, when it comes to best practice—our teams will want, not every best practice under the sun, but just the lessons of experience that are relevant to the particular work they are doing. Similarly with the bibliography: our teams will want not the whole Library of Congress, just the references and citations that are relevant to the particular project. With policies and guidelines, our teams don't need the whole massive operational manual and all the other policy guidelines that have accumulated over decades—just the sections that are relevant to the job under way. Again, with country information, our teams don't want everything we know about the countries, just the people and correspondence that lead up to the work now ongoing—in effect, the story so far. Also, they don't want all the previous reports—just the reports that had been done in the same field as the task at hand. And in signaling who are the experts, the team wants to know, not who are the gurus generally, but rather who can answer questions on key issues relevant to the particular area of work. Equally, in analytical tools, the team wants spreadsheets showing previous economic, financial, and technical analysis of earlier work in the same area, not everything that has been done.

These are the elements that the task team needs to get their work completed. These are the materials that task teams now spend weeks endeavoring to assemble, and chasing around the organization to find in paper format, often with limited success, until time runs out and they have to get on with the job without always having the proper inputs. It has always seemed an impossible dream that such materials could be assembled and made available to the team so that they could spend most of their time focusing on working with our clients and finding solutions, rather than assembling elements of the problem. But what we had always considered as so inconceivable that it wasn't even worth dreaming about is actually being implemented in a firm in Virginia just a few miles away from us.

⌣

But there is more. If we can get this far, and assemble all these elements for our own task teams, why stop there? Why not provide the same materials for our clients, who need exactly the same information and know-how for their own purposes? If we are able to assemble it for ourselves, why not share it with them? In this way, the clients can undertake more of the preparation effort—something devoutly wished by both our organization and our clients—and we can thus confine ourselves to guidance, as and when needed. In the past, the limitations and costs of communication and computing made the whole notion of such collaboration technically difficult and exorbitantly expensive. Now the plunging costs of computing and the advent of the Web mean that the constraints are no longer technical or economic. It is a question of imagination and management and willpower to make it happen.

And there is no need to confine the service to current clients. Thus suppose our professional staff share their know-how and expertise with each other and with their clients and partners and stakeholders around the world, by way of the World Wide Web. In the process, the broader audience that has no access to our expertise will suddenly be able to draw on the organization's know-how in the same way as those immediately involved in financial transactions. In this way, the organization can be useful not merely to our current financial partners, but to anyone in the entire world who is interested in economic development. Thus, the problem of coping with a vastly expanded array of clients and partners and stakeholders can be solved. As the material is assembled electronically for staff, the relevant portions can be made available for external clients at the same time.

The organization has always talked of genuine partnership with its clients and stakeholders, but has been hampered by the asymmetry of access to information. As our staff are the so-called experts, they by definition own the expertise, and it follows as night follows day that what anyone else knows must be second-best—or so the argument goes. Yet my work in Africa in trying to establish a best practice system has shown me the errors in this perspective. The impression that we have already assembled and verified the best expertise is not backed up by substance, since we have barely even begun the task of reconciling the different opinions of our individual experts into any kind of synthesis. We have good people, but the impression of always delivering the best is not systematically supported by the organization's processes. Yet if we can now assemble the best information and know-how that we have and make it directly accessible to our clients, we will not only be delivering on an operational promise. In the process, we will be creating a new era of genuine partnership.

Thus, whereas internal knowledge sharing can make us a faster and more efficient organization, external knowledge sharing has the capacity to transform it. The external dimension of knowledge sharing is the missing link. It amounts to a new kind of relationship with our existing clients and a way of coping with the potentially expanded group of partners and stakeholders who might benefit from our expertise. The idea is so far-reaching in its implications that it can lay the basis for a new corporate strategy.

⌣

When I weave these ideas into the arsenal of arguments that I am preparing and put them in slides for presentations, I find that what I am saying is capable of generating genuine excitement. As I give the presentations more frequently, I feel the momentum building, as more supporters join the cause. The idea of sharing knowledge is talked about more widely, and I find myself spending less time buttonholing individuals in the corridor and more time presenting to larger groups, as managers start inviting me to come and speak to their entire unit. I find that the presentations generate an increasingly enthusiastic response to the idea of sharing know-how.

⌣

A breakthrough comes on April 26. An enterprise-wide committee of senior managers charged with orchestrating overall organizational change invites me to give a presentation. I am dismayed when I see the agenda. A mere half-hour has been allocated to the issue of information. Worse: two other speakers have to be fitted into the same time slot, and I know that their inputs have little to do with the case I am aiming to make. So I judge that I have only ten to twelve minutes—at most fifteen—to explain a new organizational strategy and persuade the group to adopt it. A full-scale presentation is out of the question. There is only time for highlights. Most of the slides that I have been using in my regular presentations have to be sacrificed. What to include?

My choice is pragmatic, and is based on the elements that I know have elicited a strong response when I have used them in small-scale presentations.

Thus, I begin with an account of the efforts in the Africa section to set up a best practice system, showing how obvious and logical it had seemed in prospect, and how difficult it has been in implementation.

The sorry state of our information systems is quickly depicted—the huge costs, the long-unresolved problems, all so well and frequently documented.

I delineate the different businesses of the organization and point out how little support is given to the knowledge brokering function, despite very heavy investments in information systems.

> Clearly the twenty-first century is going to be different. But how? The story of the health worker in Zambia offers the possibility of viewing the future, which, I suggest, is going to be like today.
>
> Thus, in June 1995, a health worker in Kamana, Zambia, logged on to the Center for Disease Control Web site and got the answer to a question on how to treat malaria.
>
> This true story happened, not in June 2015, but in June 1995. This is not a rich country: it is Zambia, one of the least developed countries in the world. It is not even the capital of the country: it is six hundred kilometers away. But the most striking aspect of the picture is this: our

*organization isn't in it. Our organization doesn't have its know-how and expertise organized in such a way that someone like the health worker in Zambia can have access to it. But just imagine if it had!*

I sketch what it will be like to be professional using the desktop of the future, with just-in-time and just-enough material available within reach—everything one needs to get the job done.

*And if we can put all these elements in place for the task teams, why not for the clients? They have exactly the same needs as the employees. Imagine: if we do this, true partnership can emerge. Moreover, a whole group of stakeholders around the world who currently lack access to the intellectual resources of the organization will suddenly be in the picture. It will enable a different relationship with a wider group of clients and partners and stakeholders around the world. It adds up to a new organizational strategy.*

During this short presentation, I notice some positive body language. I can sense the attention and the excitement. At the conclusion, the participants come up to me quickly, to tell me how much they liked the presentation they had just heard.

"Why don't we do it?" they keep asking, "What's the next step?"

I say that we have to persuade the whole organization to accept the strategy and that not everyone is yet a believer.

"Why not?" they persist excitedly. "What's the blockage?"

The element that seems slightly strange about these exchanges is that the questions are framed as if it is *their* idea being discussed and not mine. They are speaking to me as if *they* have discovered the idea of sharing knowledge as an organizational strategy and that *I* am the one holding back progress.

I reply that I have no idea why it isn't yet going forward, although inwardly I am content that the audience has internalized the thinking to such an extent. I am asked to stay for follow-up discussions, although as it turns out, the conversation moves on to other topics.

Nevertheless, I can see that the effect of the presentation has been electric. But what is the next step? As a result of the presentation to the change management group, I now have a group of supporters at the senior level of the organization who believe that these ideas deserve a wider audience. I discover that the following week there is to be a meeting of almost the entire senior management of the organization to review the organizational change agenda. It offers a perfect opportunity to present the new thinking.

Why not? I propose the idea, but I find that there is a considerable amount of going backward and forward as to whether the topic of knowledge sharing is to be on the agenda or not. There are several other items to be covered, and there is skepticism in some quarters as to whether a presentation on information has any general relevance. Those who have heard the presentation the previous week are believers and they persist. Eventually a compromise is reached: I am to be on the agenda, but a maximum of fifteen minutes is allocated. Discussion is not to be permitted.

So a week later, on May 3, I make the presentation about knowledge sharing to almost the entire senior management of the organization.

It is the same presentation as the previous week and it seems to go just as well. There is the same positive body language and the supporters of the approach are elated, even though discussion is cut off, and hence there can be no registering of any consensus. I receive several invitations to repeat the presentation to staff in other vice-presidential units.

↬

My hope in making the presentation on May 3 is of course for a clear-cut and instantaneous decision to implement the knowledge-sharing vision across the organization. As it turns out, things are not so simple.

Although there is no open debate at the meeting itself, I learn that there is considerable debate generated in private discussions. The strategy is admittedly attractive, and there is little, if any, disagreement that this is the direction in which our organization should in due course head. But on the pace and scale of change, there is a great debate. A significant and committed phalanx of senior executives is now convinced that the vision must be pursued at once and organization-wide, building on the experience of pilot projects already under way. Others are more cautious, suggesting that we undertake more pilots and pursue an extended period of testing before plunging headlong into an across-the-board implementation of an idea that is admittedly still experimental.

For months, the debate goes on, relating not so much to the merits of the strategy itself, but rather to the different kinds of implementation arrangements that will be appropriate. Some point to the immense benefits of the change if we can get under way on a large scale. Others note the potential benefits for the existing business that are admittedly difficult to assess or measure. The complexities of implementation give everyone pause.

Some are instinctively enthusiastic and eager to proceed, admitting that there are risks but consider that these can be sorted out in the course of implementation. Others, more in the habit of looking before they leap, want to see more details of how the implementation will proceed, before making a large-scale commitment. For them, the concern is that wholesale change may be destabilizing. The differences are visceral, rather than anything that is ever explicitly articulated.

Some of the differences are attributable to attitudes in respect of technology: For some, the phenomenon of the World Wide Web creates a response of physical antipathy that is akin to what scribes in a medieval monastery must have felt on seeing a printing press for the first time and realizing what it might do to their libraries of delicately hand-painted manuscripts. For others, the Web presents a liberation, fulfilling an ancient dream of instant communication among the entire human race.

Some of the differences are also attributable to organizational perspective. Everyone is to a greater or lesser extent aware that the strategy entails a shift from an organization that has operated vertically and hierarchically to one that will operate horizontally and collaboratively across organizational borders. For some, this means deliverance. But those whose careers have flourished in mastering the vertical hierarchical pathways have a different attitude toward the shift.

Some people now see their own future, and that of the organization, in terms of the idea that has been put forward. They identify with the idea of knowledge sharing. It is no longer somebody else's idea that has been presented to them. It has become their own. They consider it to be more significant than any individual. They are convinced that organization-wide implementation has to proceed. It cannot be blocked by mere timidity. They view it as the future, their future, the organization's future. They are so energized and motivated that they keep looking for new opportunities to pursue it, no matter how much or how often the idea is attacked or mangled or satirized. For them, the idea of knowledge sharing is a beacon as to what the organization might be. In a very real sense, these people are defending their own sense of identity.

The polarization doesn't last long. By October, the struggle is over. With a small but energized phalanx of supporters at a high level of the organization, in possession of a genuinely good idea, the organization is in significant disequilibrium. Sooner, rather than later, the pieces fall into place. On October 1, 1996, at the annual meeting of the organization, the president announces the launching of an organization-wide strategy of knowledge sharing, with the proposal of a new knowledge partnership.

# TWO

# A Story That Rings True

*If we hope to live not just from moment to moment, but in true con-
sciousness of our existence, then our greatest need and most difficult
achievement is to find meaning in our lives.*

Bruno Bettelheim, *The Uses of Enchantment*[1]

February 1997. A year has passed since I was asked by the management to look into the issue of information. During that year, a movement of knowledge sharing not only has been launched across the
organization, but has now been accepted as a key strategy for the organization's future. The president has announced the organization's
commitment in the most public and irreversible way at the annual
meeting of our organization. The idea is incorporated into a strategy
document to be approved by the board of directors. Organizational
arrangements are being made for implementation. A program director
is appointed. Objectives are being set. Operations are being launched.
Budgets are being discussed. Knowledge sharing has thus been formally espoused by the organization. The game plan for managing
knowledge is official.

The knowledge-sharing strategy is depicted in a chart that captures all the elements that the management sees as key to that

---

[1] Bruno Bettelheim. *The Uses of Enchantment: The Meaning and Importance of Fairy Tales.*
New York: Knopf, 1976, p. 3.

29

strategy.[2] It delineates three phases of the process: the creation of cutting-edge knowledge, the collection of knowledge in a knowledge management system, and the application of knowledge in our different businesses. Against a night-sky background of blended blue and black, the chart glows in colors with sharp contrasts—gorgeous reds, roses, greens, and yellows. One can follow the flow of knowledge being created, then captured by the knowledge management system, and finally applied by partners, stakeholders, and clients. It simplifies the change concept into a couple of central elements. As a picture, it is worth more than a thousand words of description. With this icon in hand, we are satisfied that we have a strategy.

Despite these indicators of organizational acceptance, I can also see that much is going awry.

A task force has drafted a seventy-page report on knowledge sharing, spelling out the specifics of implementation. The report is eloquent and comprehensive. It tells everything one could want to know about the knowledge-sharing program. Yet there is little evidence that anyone *wants* to know. Hundreds of copies have been printed, but they lie in a pile in the bookcase in my office, neglected and unread.

Among the inner group of enthusiasts, there is more energy than ever. But this energy is not widespread. Despite top-level support, the momentum to implement the vision seems already to be slowing. Beyond our inner circle, there is no cohesion or focus. The bureaucratic machinery is clanking along, like some massive mechanical contraption, but we are missing the heart, the spirit, the glint in the eyes, the fire in the gut of the many individuals who will be needed to implement the vision through the long and difficult period of execution.

Now, in the depths of winter, an opportunity to relight those fires presents itself. The management has decided that the entire cadre of operational managers—several hundred men and women, the core of

---

[2] See Appendix 6.

the business administrators of the organization—are to be indoctri-
nated in the three major changes that are under way in the organization, that is to say, budget, personnel, and knowledge management.
These people are to be sorted into three groups, around seventy to a
group. On February 12, I will have forty minutes per group to make
the case for change.

It is an opportunity and a challenge. On the one hand, it is a
chance to put knowledge sharing on the managers' mental maps.
These are the people who will be needed to give their energetic support to implementation if it is to have any prospect of success. It is vital
that they see the idea in a positive light. If the presentation flops, we
will be in a difficult, if not impossible, predicament. If these managers
react badly, then it will hardly matter what the top management
decides, instructs, or commands: knowledge management in the organization will effectively be dead. All that will remain will be to arrange
a suitable funeral.

I thus have a magnificent opportunity to make the case for
knowledge management. As I get ready for the day and look back on
my earlier presentations, I can see that they will no longer serve the
purpose. For one thing, these presentations talk about decisions that
will need to be taken in the future, when in fact those decisions have
already been taken. Further, the emphasis is all on *whether* to undertake the change idea. Now the focus has to be on *how* to implement it,
giving the kind of nitty-gritty detail that I had barely even dreamed of
when I was trying to make the case for change.

Moreover, there is the problem of what to do with the story of the
Zambian health worker. This story ended up being the pivot point of
the earlier presentation, and it served the purpose of enabling audiences to visualize how knowledge sharing could function, drawing on
the experience of another organization in a context not too different
from our own. It enabled many people to grasp the basic idea of the
change idea and to visualize how it might work in their own contexts.
It was helpful in deflecting the skeptics, piquing the interest of the

cynical, turning the tolerant into sponsors, the curious into enthusiasts, allies into champions.

The Zambia story has served me well, but I sense that its shelf life has expired. It is no longer good enough to talk about what has happened in an analogous organization. I need something more immediate, something closer to home—something that shows that the approach is actually working in a real-life situation in our own organization. As I cast about the organization for possible stories, I find many that come close to being suitable, but none has the magic of that story from Zambia. There is always some distracting element that could end up in generating a discussion about the facts of the story itself, rather than greater understanding of the phenomenon of knowledge sharing. Or the story is incomplete and fails to convey the full amplitude of the strategy. I wander around the organization, looking at example after example, pursuing leads from all over, and still, there is nothing that meets my need. I feel like a Hollywood film studio executive who keeps rejecting story after story because it is "not quite right for us," and in the end, arriving at a situation where there are no stories left to make the film. Unlike the studio executive, I don't have the luxury of waiting until the right story comes along. The presentation is scheduled for February 12. It is going to take place whether I am ready or not.

In desperation, I go back to the rejection pile and come across a story that at least partly serves my purpose.

*A leader of one of the multidisciplinary task teams was in Santiago, Chile, when our client contacted her and asked: Quick, what is the experience of your organization in other countries in dealing with the demands of school teachers? As it happened, the task team didn't have the full answer to the question on hand. So the team contacted the advisory service of the education network, which was able to assemble experiences from staff working in other countries around the world that were analogous to the situation of Chile.*

*The material was sent to Santiago electronically, the team was able to synthesize the material, and in a matter of hours, the client had the answer—a feat that would have been impossible without having the advisory service make the connections between the team and the other staff working on similar issues in other countries. The client was delighted with the responsiveness, and the transaction led to an intensified collaboration in the sector.*

The story is good in that it demonstrates how the team was able to connect with the other experts in the domain of education. What it doesn't do, however, is to illustrate a key feature of our knowledge-sharing strategy: that is, how we will collect valuable materials and make them available both internally to other staff, and in due course, externally to clients, partners, and stakeholders around the world, in the same way that the Centers for Disease Control had made available the know-how for diagnosing and treating malaria, and so provided a solution for the health worker in Zambia on the other side of the planet.

What to do?

I extrapolate.

In the absence of a story on hand that illustrates the full array of the change strategy, I use the true story as far as it goes, and then say: let's imagine. Let's continue the story the way it should unfold, assuming that everything proceeds the way it is meant to in our proposed knowledge-sharing strategy.

So the story continues on an explicitly extrapolated basis.

*What will happen in the future? What we have learned from the Chile experience is now recognized as being valuable. The material can be edited for further reuse and entered into the knowledge base, so that when a new client with similar problems, say, a country in Africa, asks another task team for the global experience in this area, the answer is readily accessible through the organization's Intranet.*

*This will only happen if three conditions are in place: first, if there is a classification system that enables one to find the Chile synthesis in a large knowledge base; secondly, if the education advisory service has an easy-to-contact human being who can answer questions and guide the search; and thirdly, if there is institutional technology platform that makes it easy to find things across organizational boundaries.*

*So, as the story continues, the African experience will be edited for further reuse and entered into the knowledge base. Inputs from other parts of the organization—and outside—can be added.*

*Later on, when the system is fully developed, and the expertise is made available externally, when yet another client—say, from Asia— has a question in the same area, there are new possibilities. The client can go into the knowledge base on its own through the World Wide Web, find the Chile synthesis, find the African synthesis, find the other inputs, and then either use them on its own, or ask for assistance in applying them to its local situation. In this way, the know-how is made available quickly, inexpensively, for all the world to use.*

~

The morning of February 12 is cold. Under a beautiful crisp blue sky, an icy, biting wind greets anyone who ventures outside. The looks on the faces of the managers who file into the conference room that morning are precisely the looks—tight-lipped, skeptical, grim—that you would expect to see on people who have been taken from the workplace on a wintry morning, gathered together in three batches, and asked to sit through a series of presentations on the changes that the top management has decided will take place in the organization at this time. If some of the audience have heard about knowledge management, most have not paid much attention to it. The very term "knowledge management" seems a strange contradiction in terms. I imagine the questions swirling through their minds. "Can knowledge be managed? What is knowledge, anyway? Is this the new management fad? Meanwhile, what new crises are building up in the in-box back in my office?" These are not people who have arrived with any sense of positive excitement to be here this morning, listening to my presentation. They have come because they have been instructed to come. Their objective? Most likely, to be on their way at the earliest diplomatic opportunity, while finding out how this strange, cockamamie thing called knowledge management—that has apparently been decided by someone high up in the organization—might end up affecting them.

It is an unpromising audience, but not too different from the audiences that one inevitably faces when launching major change in any organization. They have other things on their minds. They have other on-going priorities. They are busy. They are worried. They are already coping with a lot of disruption and turbulence. They would not have freely chosen to spend their morning this way.

If I had the time to talk to each of them, I might be able to instigate a dialogue, find out about their current problems and objectives, and then discuss how the substance of what I am presenting—the sharing of knowledge—might in fact be helpful in dealing with the issues that they are confronting. But there is no time for that. There are hundreds of them, each coming to the session with a different set of issues. They work in different geographical regions, have different professional backgrounds, and are facing a bewildering array of different problems.

The presentation that I have prepared to tackle the challenge begins with the now-official chart of knowledge sharing. It shows how knowledge will flow, in the new set of arrangements, from one part of the organization to another. It then goes on to tell the story of the task team in Chile. How a task team leader in Chile actually used the approach of knowledge sharing to serve a client's needs better and quicker than would otherwise have been possible. How the client was delighted. How, if we extrapolate the story just a little, we can see how the approach could be even more efficient and effective by enabling direct access to knowledge collections that we will build up over time. Supporting presentations from staff working in some of the pilot projects of knowledge sharing (statistics, private sector infrastructure, education) are in the same vein: practical accounts of what they are actually doing and how the change idea is beginning to operate.

After the introductory chart defining knowledge management, the presentation is a set of stories, illustrating how the change idea is being implemented. But the gist of it is also an invitation: an invitation for each member of the audience to imagine what knowledge sharing could be like in the context of his or her own work, context, and problems. Since each person's work and context and problems are different, no presentation can conceivably deal with them all. Instead, what we do is to offer some illustrations of how knowledge sharing is *already* working—and could, with a little extrapolation, work in future—and so spark collaborative and constructive thinking in the audience as to how it might help them.

As the presentations proceed, we see the body language of the audience becoming more positive. Arms unfold. The odd smile unwinds. The atmosphere relaxes. At the end of each session, when we finish our presentations, the questions are generally constructive and positively oriented toward understanding how knowledge sharing might operate and how one might make it work in other contexts. We—the presenters—feel that the presentation has gone very well. Knowledge sharing was the segment of the briefing sessions that had evoked the most advance skepticism. But we are not entirely surprised when we see a few weeks later the results of the audience surveys, which show that our session was rated as most informative and helpful.

By contrast, the parallel sessions on budget and personnel proceedings were conducted in a question-and-answer format. I learn that at these sessions, the questions dwelt on problems, and so the sessions tended to leave a fuzzy, negative impression.

During the succeeding weeks, we are invited to show the presentation with the Chile story on several occasions to the top management, and eventually the board of directors, where it enjoys commensurate success. Thereafter it is repeated to many other groups throughout the organization, and beyond.

I am pleased with the evident success of the presentation. What is an even greater relief to me is that in all these many presentations no one ever stands up and objects to the imaginary aspects of the Chile story. I explicitly state on each occasion that the story about what happened after the initial advice to our client is an extrapolation of what had happened: the capturing of the know-how and its insertion into the knowledge base, so that it would be accessible by way of the Web either internally or externally, has not yet happened, but is expected to happen. Each time I make the presentation, I hold my breath, expecting at any second someone to fling a sharp-edged question as to whether we could possibly rely on a mere tale, a story, a myth of what *might* happen as the serious basis for betting our organization's future. But the question never comes. Instead, the Chile story serves its purpose of opening up many people's minds to what the future might be like. The audience is so busy exploring the concept of knowledge sharing, inventing their own futures within it, and adjusting their own new identities to this knowledge-sharing future that even the most skeptical of listeners never get around to objecting either to the slenderness of the evidence or to its imaginary character. The story has served its purpose in successfully catapulting the minds of this somewhat difficult audience forward to a conceptual destiny that they are happily helping to invent.

What I have stumbled upon in the Chile story—and the Zambia story before it—is thus a story that provides the kind of plausibility, coherence, and reasonableness that enables people to make sense of immensely complex changes that are being discussed. The story holds the disparate elements together long enough to energize and guide action, plausibly enough to allow people to make retrospective sense of whatever happens, and engagingly enough that they will contribute their own input into creating the future of the organization.[3]

It doesn't seem to matter that the second half of the Chile story is extrapolated. What is more important is that the story creates meaning for the audience and helps them to order in their minds a complex set of phenomena about the arrangements and changes that are being proposed in the organization. These audiences of highly

---

[3] Karl E. Weick and Larry D. Browning, "Argument and Narration in Organizational Communication," *Yearly Review of Management of the Journal of Management*, edited by J.G. Hund and J.D. Blair (1986), Vol. 12, No. 2, pp. 243–259, at page 250.

sophisticated and educated managers accept the explicit fiction without question, and indeed seem grateful for the sense that it generates, rather than quibbling over its imaginary character. The story in effect helps them connect with a world in which they can see meaning.

For the story to be effective in this sense, the critical issue is not so much, Is it true? or, Is it accurate? or, Did it happen exactly that way? so much as, Does the story ring true?

When we say that a story rings true, we are not so much saying that it is true in a scientific sense (i.e., is there evidence of generalizations that could be proved by experiment?) or in a legal sense (i.e., is it the best explanation of the admissible factual evidence?), but rather asking, does it possess narrative rationality? We are asking: is it a reasonable and believable account of the elements? Is it one that tends to make sense?

When the story rings true, it enables the listeners to generate a new gestalt in their minds, which embraces the main point of the change. For beyond the obvious transmittal of information, the immersion of the self in the events that constitute the story can have an impact. To follow a story as a listener is to give a kind of implicit consent, to exhibit a willingness to participate in a conceptual journey, leading to a mental destination that at the outset is unknown to the listener.

The fact that, with a story, some listeners miss certain details about the change idea, or do not catch fully all the implications of the change, isn't necessarily significant. Change ideas in large organizations tend to be so complicated that full communication of the ideas in their entirety is not even theoretically possible. The ideas themselves are not precise and are generally still evolving, so that they cannot be captured or even fully understood at any one point in time during conception and implementation. Incompleteness of communication is inevitable.

Completeness of communication however is not necessary. The overriding goal of this particular kind of communication is to generate in the listener's mind a big-picture idea that will strike the listener not only as fresh but also as self-generated, so that it will become part of the way in which the listeners see their lives and work and the identity of the organization in which they work. The fresh idea is not one that pre-exists and is simply being transmitted. An idea cannot easily enter into the listeners' basic perceptual framework as a fresh idea through which they view the world, unless they themselves co-create it. For this purpose, a story that rings true can be a useful tool.4

---

4 See Roman Jakobson, "Linguistics and Poetry," in *Style in Language,* edited by Thomas A. Sebeok. Cambridge Technology Press of Massachusetts Institute of Technology, 1960, pp. 350–377. Discussed in Donald E. Polkinghorne, *Narrative Knowing and the Human Sciences* Albany N.Y. State University of New York Press, 1988, pp. 33–34.

# THREE

# Communicating a Vision

*Contrary to the ancient myth, wisdom does not burst forth fully devel-
oped like Athena out of Zeus's head; it is built up, small step by small
step, from most irrational beginnings.*

Bruno Bettelheim, *The Uses of Enchantment*[1]

The contrast between organizations as they appear in management
textbooks, and organizations as we encounter them in real life, has frequently been remarked.[2] In textbooks, the organization is often made
to seem like a piece of well-greased machinery. Everybody who works
in the organization knows what it is all about and is concerned prin-
cipally with implementing its mission. People get satisfaction from
their work. Anxiety is low and morale is on the up-and-up. People
interact with each other in frictionless, mutually supportive teams.
Any troublemakers are quickly ditched. If there are any managerial
difficulties, they are essentially technical questions, whose resolution
lies in applying the correct techniques of management that inevitably
are those being recommended by that particular textbook.

The organizations that we experience in real life often seem to us
to be the opposite. Everything seems to be falling rapidly apart.

---

[1] Bruno Bettelheim. *The Uses of Enchantment: The Meaning and Importance of Fairy Tales.*
New York: Knopf, 1976, p. 3.

[2] A particularly clear formulation of the contrast may be found in Howard S. Schwartz,
*Narcissistic Process and Corporate Decay: The Theory of the Organizational Ideal.* New
York: New York University Press, 1990.

People's main preoccupation is to see that it doesn't fall on them. A situation not far from chaos reigns. Nobody really knows what is going on. Everybody wants to know what is going on, because there is immense risk in ignorance. Structures seem to get in the way of implementing the organization's mission, yet increasingly frequent reorganizations do not seem to lead to forward progress. Budgets are cut in the very areas where funding is needed. Anxiety and stress are prevalent. People are uneasy in dealing with each other, since no one is quite sure about anyone else's true agenda. People hesitate to point out a problem lest it be considered their fault. Management issues are intractable, and managers feel that they have done well if they have been able to make it through the day.

What is less generally recognized is that both situations may often prevail in the same organization at the same time.

Thus, in September 1997, when I come back from summer vacation and return to work, I find myself at the epicenter of an exciting change program. It is like a complex life form that continues to evolve in surprising ways. There is widespread energy and optimism.

The program enjoys most of the textbook elements of success—all of the things that I aimed to put in place when I had set out on this quest. Explicit goals. Corporate endorsement. Programs. Budgets. Staff. Governance structures. It is a huge new movement that corresponds in high degree to what I wanted and proposed. We are proceeding according to the book.

The program swirls around me in humming, buzzing, blooming growth. We are experiencing a dizzying and thrilling sense of fulfillment, as a buoyant sense of forward progress pulses through our veins, enlivens our meetings, and drives us with the idea of creating a new kind of organization. We are dazzled and humbled by the challenge of the work—as if imagining for an instant that the invention of the next century depends on us. The teams come together easily and bristle with new thinking. It is hard not to see morale as thriving, on a very positive trend. There is external recognition. It is life as I want it to be.

Yet behind these scenes and beneath the surface of this exemplary order, a different story is unfolding, a story of dark and bewildering contrasts.

True, a new life form has been spawned inside the organization—knowledge sharing—but it is agonizingly fragile and precarious, like some newly emergent creature washed up on the shores of evolution. Its prospects are limited and pitiful, as it is liable to be crushed in a harsh Darwinian struggle with other life forms in a bitter struggle for survival.

As I look at the underlying reasons for its fragility, I recognize to my horror that essential elements of the basic change idea have been omitted. These are not insignificant details at the periphery, but elements that are absolutely central to our eventual success. One of the most important concerns communities of practice. We can see that the program is only making progress where the employees have formed themselves into communities or groups of practitioners where there is a safe space for knowledge sharing. These communities were not a formal part of the original plan, and yet they need to be there. We must have been thinking—to the extent that we gave the matter any thought at all—that the communities would somehow create themselves spontaneously. Now the reality is apparent: far from emerging spontaneously, these communities do not emerge on their own. In fact, the more we talk about them, the more we realize how few people know what we were talking about. We had assumed something fundamental, and it simply doesn't exist.

How can we trigger such non-hierarchical groupings or communities into existence in some organic fashion? It is evident that it will be useless to issue an edict for these communities to form themselves, even if we could think of a suitable instruction—which, as it happens, we cannot. It will be self-contradictory to issue a hierarchical command to employees to organize themselves in a non-hierarchical manner. We—the organizers—hardly know what these communities are, or what they will look like, or how they will function, or what resources they will need. We have heard about such communities in other organizations. We have a few examples in front of us, already existing, but they usually seem peculiar to the individuals that constitute them. For the most part, the people we expected to be setting up these communities don't have a clue. Yet we suspect that without the communities, the program will falter and fail. Why weren't they part of the original program? Why hadn't we thought of them and made some arrangement for them? The need for the communities has been staring us in the face from the outset. All of the literature suggests that they are essential. Yet as we look around, we see that we have made no formal provision for them. In our desperate struggle to get the program launched, we have omitted the quintessence. It is as if we have designed a living creature, but failed to provide its heart.

Just as fundamental, the lifeblood of the program—money—has been effectively cut off. An ostensibly generous amount of money was earmarked in the budget to fund knowledge-sharing activities across the organization, but for a whole set of complicated reasons, accessing the funding is proving difficult, and often practically impossible. What should be a flow is no more than a trickle. There are suspicions that the money is being diverted to other purposes.

As we confront these conundrums, we realize that even internally our movement of knowledge sharing is not completely cohesive. It isn't just the skeptics. Even our genuine friends and enthusiasts cannot be counted on to be responsive to any central direction. The very spirit of knowledge sharing is non-hierarchical, and this means that those attracted to it are those who are less amenable to any sort of superintendence. This tendency in turn risks leading to multiple breakaway movements. People are less interested in the overall program than in having autonomy to do their own thing. Top-level attention to knowledge sharing is not always centered on critical issues.

An external observer could perhaps sense that the organization is once again polarizing into supporters and opponents, along with the usual chorus of bystanders and armchair skeptics. Since the formal adoption of the knowledge-sharing program, the most explicit and vociferous critics have gone underground where they are now beginning to stimulate an undercurrent of second-guessing—perhaps more insidious and risky for the program than explicit opposition. The organization is thus in that delicate and difficult stage of a change program when the costs and dislocations of a major change are all too apparent, but the benefits are not yet evident. Is our flight plan still valid? Has someone in the control tower blundered? Is it all a terrible error? It is a crisis of a kind, with the risk of a loss of confidence, the kind of crisis that is perhaps typical at this stage of change.

Worst of all, despite the governance structure, nothing is under anyone's direct control. No orders can be given to fix things. Everything depends on persuasion and exhortation. There is no ostensible authority to instruct anyone to do anything. We have always said that vertical structures and hierarchy are the problem, not the solution. And yet without these mechanical contraptions, our situation risks drifting toward a state of chaos. I begin to wonder whether the whole undertaking will be possible at all without some degree of control. Would it not be easier if the program had a hierarchical overseer—a Napoleonic overlord to call the shots, and in the process, quickly and directly solve the problems? Would such an approach be compatible with the collaborative character of knowledge sharing?

And so it is the best of times, the worst of times—crazy times with a thrill a minute. We never know what is going to happen next. Mirage and chimera. Are we succeeding or failing? We wonder: "If this is success, what must failure be like?"

The main elements that must be addressed are clear enough. We have to invent the communities of practice and stimulate them into existence. We have to explain the concept of communities of practice to people who are still struggling to understand the elements of the program and to get their enthusiastic buy-in. We also have to recover the effective use of the budget and get it to go where it needs to go—to the communities of practice.

Even more important: we have to regenerate fresh energy, and build new commitment. We have to get most folks moving down the main road, instead of in the gravel and ditches, or wandering through the forest.

But how?

I ponder these issues for some months. There is a hiatus in major presentations and so I have plenty of time for reflection. I patiently await the day when I will have a chance to set matters straight. In preparation for such a day, I periodically review the presentations that I had been making both inside and outside the organization. These presentations seem impeccable. I have been using the Chile story as the principal instrument, and this always seems to work.

But the presentations are also full of charts that are not in story form. Charts with arrows and boxes and two-by-two matrices, which show the ebb and flow of knowledge sharing. I feel justifiable pride in these charts. They have satisfied the management and have become institutional icons. They are shown on multiple posters displayed in the organization's corridors and hallways. They have also attained a certain notoriety outside the organization. They are reproduced by journals and other organizations, and disseminated around the world. The widespread acceptance encourages me to think: they must be good and effective.

But as the year wears on, an uneasiness has begun to creep into my thinking. I have found myself hurrying through the chart section of the presentation so that I can get to the story, and linger there a while, and stretch it out, even if only for a few seconds. I can sense the audience's response to the narrative, just as I can sense their inertness during the definition section of the presentation. And yet I don't change my approach. It is so obvious to me that I have to define the change idea in analytical terms with the official chart that the thought never occurs to me that I have any other option.

But clearly the chart now has to change. Key elements are missing. The communities of practice are totally absent. The chart is no help on the budget issues, or other questions that are tormenting us. At the very least, we will need a new chart that encompasses the solutions to the new challenges. And so I begin working on new charts, and new visual representations.

In version after version, I explore ways of depicting the elements. But I come across a dilemma for which I can see no resolution. When I add new elements to the existing chart with more arrows and boxes, the already-complicated picture becomes even more difficult to follow. The more correctly it specifies all the elements, the less intelligible it becomes. When I start again with a totally different chart, it immediately seems unfamiliar and strange, and I find myself having to explain why the overall framework has changed. The chart seems to have become the problem rather than the solution. I am deeply puzzled and have no idea what to do.

These are the issues I am pondering when I attend a conference in Charleston in November 1997. At the conference, I find myself one morning listening to a celebrated speaker in the field explain his chart of knowledge sharing.

I have seen the chart that is on the screen this morning many times before, since I have read the presenter's book, one of the leading works in the field.[3] Even so, I find myself struggling to understand the chart. Here I am, already practicing the very process of knowledge sharing that the chart is trying to describe, and I am having difficulties following it. Imagine what a newcomer must be feeling! I can also see that a large part of the talk this morning is spent in trying to explain the implications of the chart. The chart is so complicated that the explanations go on for many minutes, as the speaker walks us through all the implications in ever-increasing detail. Nothing clicks for me. Nothing sings. Nothing resonates. I feel as if I am back in grade school trying to understand an esoteric lesson in differential cal-

---

3 Ikujiro Nonaka and Hirotaka Takeuchi. *The Knowledge-Creating Company: how Japanese Companies Create the Dynamics of Innovation.* New York: Oxford University Press, 1995.

culus. What is so clear and evident to the speaker is almost incomprehensible to me, even though as a fellow practitioner I am following in some general intellectual sense every step of the logic that he is trying to get across. But I cannot envisage using the chart to do anything or analyze anything. It is not something that I instinctively memorize or that becomes a part of my mental framework. It is there like an unintelligible Rosetta stone, an artifact with strange languages carved on it. At best, it is as useful as a logarithmic table that I might keep with me, to refer to when I am confronted with a difficult issue.

I can see that the speaker is being generous in giving us, the audience, the very thought processes that have enabled him to understand what is happening in a situation of knowledge transfer. He is doing this with incredible honesty and comprehensiveness, and to help, he has encapsulated these thought processes in a slide with arrows and boxes. The problem is that generosity and honesty are not enough. His thought processes don't coincide with mine. The more pride and excitement that he shows in explaining his chart, the more frustration and inadequacy I feel, since I don't resonate with anything he is saying.

Then the thought dawns on me: this is how my listeners must feel when they look at my charts with arrows and boxes and matrices. While I am waxing lyrical and going on poetically about the implications of this arrow or that box, the audience is thinking: what is he burbling on about? It is at this moment that the penny finally drops for me: the chart isn't helping at all. The chart—and the time spent on explaining it—is the problem, not the solution.

I can see immediately that I have to drop the chart from my own presentation. But how? If I give no definition of the overall change program, how will people grasp what I am talking about? Haven't thinkers since Aristotle agreed that one should begin by defining terms? Is it possible that I should put all my eggs in the storytelling basket? Moreover, the official chart on knowledge sharing has become an institutional icon. The management has come to understand it. It is published around the world. Surely people will think it a critical omission if it is just dropped? Is it worth taking the risk, to throw away the intellectual scaffolding that supports the change idea I am promoting and rely entirely on a story to get the message across?

The opportunity soon presents itself to test this line of thinking.

In December, to settle the organizational unrest, an open house meeting is called by the senior management in a large auditorium. The meeting is advertised widely. It is the biggest internal audience I have ever addressed, comprising a slice of the senior management and a couple of hundred staff. It is a make-or-break occasion, and crucial for the future of the knowledge-sharing program.

I haven't come this far without taking risks, and the logic seems irresistible. So I prepare a presentation that begins with a story from Yemen with no charts explaining or defining what we are talking about, except the story.

*In July 1997, we had a task team in Yemen, a country in the Middle East and one of the poorest countries in the world. The team was working with a client on an education project and was coming to the end of its visit.*

*Then something unexpected happened. The client asked for some urgent advice. It wanted to know what it should do about building an information system for its education services. As it happened, the members of the task team didn't happen to have this particular expertise either in their heads or in their briefcases.*

*So the team contacted the staff of the help desk of the education sector, who were in touch with the community of practice in the education sector. They were able to ascertain that the best and most relevant piece of expertise on this subject was in Kenya, in Africa, where similar work had been done, along with a critique of its strengths and weaknesses. The results of the Kenya work were then faxed to Yemen so that within a forty-eight hour time frame the task team could be sitting down with the client and discussing the solution to the problem.*

*Without the organization's knowledge-sharing program, things would have happened very differently. The task team would have told the client that they would get back to him, and then would have gone on to another country, in this case Jordan. Eventually, the team would have got back to Washington and—let's assume they remembered— would have searched for and found the answer, and dispatched it to Yemen. The answer would have got there within weeks, rather than days, and the team would not have been present to discuss it with the client.*

*Nor does the approach stop with merely satisfying the individual client. Now that we have established that the Kenya expertise is valuable, it can be edited for reuse and entered into the electronic knowledge base, so that when other staff in the organization face a similar problem, they can find it by way of the organization's intranet.*

*Moreover, when external access is established, clients would be able to find the answer directly on the Web if they so desire. There is a dramatic acceleration of cycle time in providing advice from what used to be weeks, to a matter of minutes.*

*Although the magic of technology is enabling this to happen rapidly, what underlies the transformation are people—people operating in communities of practice where sharing is the normal way of operating, so that when the request comes from Yemen, there is a human community in place that enables the help desk to find precisely the right piece of expertise.*

The presentation goes on to explain the various components of the program, but always in relation to the story of Yemen.

The response to the presentation is overwhelmingly positive. The questions are relevant and supportive and focused on how to make the changes happen. People can see the meaning of the community of practice. There is electricity in the air. There is excitement. People are energized.

Of all the hundreds of people who see the presentation, not a single one ever asks whatever happened to the official chart with its arrows and boxes showing the flow of knowledge. It isn't just that no one *misses* it. No one even *remembers* it. It has disappeared into a black hole of oblivion as if it never existed—perhaps the inevitable fate of all unnatural, manufactured, inanimate artifacts.

The presentation with the Yemen story is repeated on many occasions over the succeeding months. On each occasion, there is the same generation of positive energy. We are back on track.

What is amazing to me is that the success in communicating the idea of knowledge sharing, including the idea of the community of practice, and in re-energizing a huge group of people comes not from crafting a superior chart, but rather from throwing the chart aside and simply telling a story. I have stopped talking in terms of multicolored boxes on night-black sky with arrows flashing from part of the matrix to another. Instead I am telling a story about people who have lived the knowledge-sharing idea and how things happened in a real-life situation. The difficulties of communication seem to dissolve. A complicated concept is being communicated by a story.

The presentation is easier to deliver. I no longer have to explain what the boxes are and what is in them. I am talking about people, real people, from within the organization—people who are known, who can be talked to, and who can explain whether this is the way it actually happened.

And the presentation is easier to listen to. It is more interesting. It is simpler to follow. Hearing the idea of knowledge sharing in relation to a story makes everything come to life. We are learning about people and what they said, and did and how it led to their success. Suddenly everything is more easily discussed and understood.

And so I begin to ask myself what is going on here. Previously, I have been using stories to support the analytical framework for change. I have been assuming that the main work of explanation is being done by the analytical scaffolding. Now I have taken away most of the analytical scaffolding and the story is doing almost all the work on its own. On its own the story is just as successful, if not more so, than when the analytical scaffolding was present. How could this be possible?

I have been brought up, and educated for decades, to think that analytical reasoning is the epitome of thinking, and that stories are of no more than secondary importance. I am convinced that any success that I have achieved at school is rooted in my ability to think analytically—to see the relations between concepts and to be able to explain them. A similar experience in my working life has confirmed the same world view. Analytical is good; anecdotal is bad. I know that the world of science and enlightenment emerged from an era of darkness where there was dependence on myth and fairy tale and anecdote. It is self-evident that we have entered the more reliable world of science and logic and verification through experiment. The greatest material progress that the world has ever seen has occurred because we have put storytelling behind us. Instead, we have built our world on the rigor of scientific thinking. These are such fundamental assumptions that it is difficult for me even to imagine any alternative, let alone call the assumptions into question.

And yet here, in my day-to-day living, I am confronted with unmistakable signs of the opposite phenomenon. The more I concentrate on the analytics, the more I run into difficulty and resistance. The more I put the analytic thinking to one side and instead put forward the story, the easier things seem to be. These questions race through my mind in a disorienting fashion. Is everything that I have been raised and educated to believe, and have faith in, wrong? What on earth is going on?

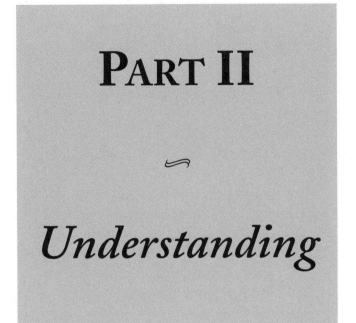

# PART II

## Understanding

# FOUR

# Getting Inside an Idea

*If truth is a chosen narrative, then new stories, new aesthetics, are also new truths.*

Jane Hirshfield, *Nine Gates*[1]

**I**mmediately after the open house meeting in which I use the Yemen story to explain knowledge management without the scaffolding of abstract analysis, I grab my bags, make a dash in a taxi for Dulles airport, and board a plane for a conference in London where I am to make a presentation. As the plane lumbers down the runway and then ascends into the air, I feel as if all the issues, problems, and forces with which I have been struggling inside the organization are beginning to dwindle into insignificance far below me on the ground. I settle into my seat for the compressed nighttime of a transatlantic flight, and take out a book that I have brought with me for the journey. The first sentence reads:

> *It was Virginia Woolf who started me thinking about thinking again, set me to weighing the relative merits of the abstract analytical mode that fueled the writing of these essays against the attractions of a more oblique and subjective approach.*[2]

---

[1] Jane Hirshfield, *Nine Gates: Entering the Mind of Poetry.* New York: HarperCollins, 1997, p. 5.

[2] Sven Birkerts, *The Gutenberg Elegies: The Fate of Reading in an Electronic Age.* Boston: Faber and Faber, 1994, p. 11.

The words set my mind whirling. Certainly they bear on the issues with which I am wrestling. But oblique? And subjective? I have been trained for decades to believe that such orientations are anathema, approaches to be shunned, not embraced. Surely, objective is better than subjective and direct is better than oblique? Had not Aristotle in ancient Greece several thousand years ago established these basics?

> [L]et us lay down that the virtue of style is to be clear, (since a speech is a kind of indication; if it does not indicate clearly, it will not be performing its function).[3]

The book is written by a literary essayist called Sven Birkerts. It is the kind of unscientific work that I have been educated to despise. Equally, in the circles in which I work, anything literary is the epitome of the flimsy and the trivial. I have selected Birkerts's book for the flight because I have told myself that I want to plunge deeper into the meaning of storytelling, though what exactly I am looking for, I don't really know. I am unsure that the essays of a writer who detests technology can offer anything helpful to a practitioner of knowledge management, in which the use of technology is central. And yet, my own recent experience tells me that science and analysis cannot be the entire story. And so I read on.

Birkerts quotes a selection from Virginia Woolf's *A Room of One's Own:*

> Here then was I . . . sitting on the banks of a river a week or two ago in fine October weather, lost in thought. . . . To the right and left bushes of some sort, golden and crimson, glowed with the colour, even if it seemed burnt with the heat, of fire. On the further bank willows wept in perpetual lamentation, their hair about their shoulders. . . . There one might have sat the clock round lost in thought. Thought—to call it

---

3 Aristotle, *The Art of Rhetoric*, translated by H.C. Lawson-Tancred. London: Penguin Books, 1991, Section 9, Chapter 3.2, p. 218.

*a prouder name than it deserved—let its line down into the stream. It swayed, minute after minute, hither and thither among the reflections and the weeds, letting the water lift it and sink it, until—you know the little tug—the sudden conglomeration of an idea at the end of one's line: and then the cautious hauling of it in, and the careful laying of it out? Alas, laid on the grass how small, how insignificant this thought of mine looked: the sort of fish that a good fisherman puts back into the water so that it may grow fatter and be one day worth cooking and eating.*[4]

As I lay the book down to take a mouthful from the glass of red wine that the dark-haired flight attendant helpfully provides, memories of my student days at Oxford University come flooding back to me. Two years of study, drinking warm beer in pubs in winter, shivering in incompletely heated rooms, slumbering through lovely summers, suffering the incessantly wet weather generating unbelievably green lawns, walking past dark and tangled shrubbery, seeing honeysuckle and clematis running up the mullions of oriel windows, with musk and noisette roses fixing themselves in moldering crevices of old stone, masses of hollyhocks springing up from massed banks of flowers, walled gardens with impeccably clipped hedges of box and yew—the memories are as fresh as yesterday.

I hardly know now whether I am hurtling through the air above the northeast seaboard of America at more than five hundred miles an hour, or sitting motionless on a river bank beneath weeping willows in England, in the company Virginia Woolf and Sven Birkerts, fishing for fresh thoughts in a pool of memories.

I have heard that to change one's place is to change one's nature. It is a happy accident to be on my way to England, the country that

---

[4] Virginia Woolf, *A Room of One's Own*. New York: The Fountain Press; London: The Hogarth Press, 1929; reprint, San Diego: Harcourt Brace & Company, 1989, p. 5. Quoted by Sven Birkerts, in *The Gutenberg Elegies: The Fate of Reading in an Electronic Age*. Boston: Faber and Faber, 1994, p. 12.

invented the idiosyncratic miracle that we know as the English language. Perhaps the perfect place to be pondering the magic of narrative.

From my student days, I remember the general preference of the English for case law over legislation, their partiality for the particular ahead of the general. It is a country that, even today, is governed by no written constitution, preferring instead the practice of prior generations. The English are by character resistant to grand abstractions. They instinctively prefer the quirky, the individual, the nicks and marks and hollows and crannies that permit one to get a purchase on the world, a reading on reality's coordinates. The intense granularity and particularity of experience are generally uppermost in their minds.

Even so great a mathematician as Sir Isaac Newton stands out as a national anomaly. His discovery of calculus in 1665 was published only forty years later, by which time a Continental mathematician, Leibniz, had already paved the way. Indeed, it was the recognition generated by Newton's practical invention of a telescope with a parabolic mirror eliminating spherical aberration that made him famous. Recognition of his mathematics came later.

Now memories of real characters mix together with the fictitious Mr. Pickwick and Rosalind and King Lear, in a strange blend in my brain. These people seem as real to me as the memories of the not-very-well-kempt fellow students I knew at university, rushing from tutorial to the Bodleian library, clutching law books and folders, wearing beige or gray trench coats or jackets, shoulders perpetually hunched over, as if to miss the spitting rain.

As my plane races over the ocean and across the midnight sky, my mind returns to Sven Birkerts and his nostalgic, impassioned, heartfelt plea for the pleasures of reading, along with his thundering denunciation of the digital world of television and the World Wide Web into which the author perceives himself as having been plunged against his will. While Birkerts seems to me utterly wrong-headed and befuddled in his instinctive funk when it comes to issues of technology, he is nevertheless refreshingly honest and eloquent in his sincerity. And eventually, he is able to land a very significant fish, by describing with magnificent exactitude the experience of reading a story.[5]

When readers follow a story, Birkerts suggests, they journey—virtually—with the storyteller into a different world. Implicitly the readers project themselves with the storyteller into a different mental location—the place where the story takes place—even though they have never physically left their static sitting position. The imagined reality to which they pass is a world elicited by a creator who, as a kind of sponsoring god, uses linguistic and other tools to stimulate this world into existence. The world might exist vividly or dimly, depending on the storyteller's skill and the readers' interest. This new mental location, generated by the story, is held in suspension by the intent of the storyteller as well as through the participation of the readers. The readers help invent this virtual world, along with the story line provided by the narrator. Listening to a story is thus not simply an issue of registering the imprint of the storyteller's words. The storyteller's words are the stimulus for the creation of this virtual world, but it is the readers whose participation contributes to conjuring it up.

The transition of the readers from their physical existence, in which they are then living, to the virtual or imagined world, the space where the story occurs in their minds, can be gradual or rapid. If the storyteller has the readers' full attention and can refer to a world with which the readers are intimately familiar, they can be transported quite quickly to the new mental habitat. If by contrast the story is about a world with which the readers have little or no familiarity and to which the storyteller can make no direct analogy, then the storyteller might have to spend significant time and effort helping the readers create in their minds the traits of the new domain.

What occurs when the transit is successful is an immersion of the readers in whole or in part in a different world, in which they hand over their groundedness in the here-and-now to project their new

---

5 Sven Birkerts, *The Gutenberg Elegies: The Fate of Reading in an Electronic Age.* Boston: Faber and Faber, 1994, pp. 80–82.

existence in the mental elsewhere of the story. The more fully the readers can accomplish this transition, the more effective the story is as a story.

As I read Birkerts's book, I see that it is explicitly limited to what happens when people *read* a story. Yet it is immediately obvious to me, given the puzzle that I am struggling to understand, that Birkerts's description of the experience of following a story is not limited to reading a story, as Birkerts contends. The process he successfully delineates applies more generally to *all* forms of storytelling.

When I tell the story of Zambia, or Chile, or Yemen, it is plausible to think that while the listeners remain physically present in the tawdry, ill-furnished conference room in which I am talking, mentally they are far away, traveling in my company, in a wholly different mental reality. When the storytelling is successful, the room in which I am talking will be dimming in the listener's mind, so that the world of the health worker in Zambia, or the task team in Chile or in Yemen, can take on an outline and a definite presence.

Another fascinating aspect of Birkerts's depiction is the insight that the process by which the transition from physical to virtual worlds happens is active, and not at all passive. The readers are energetically conniving and conspiring with the storyteller all the time. Birkerts suggests that readers will that the world where the story occurs should come into existence. They project themselves into that world and enter it as through a turnstile. They can often do this with astonishing facility, he says, as though they seem in some way to need it. Readers in the grip of an effective story tend to forget—for the duration of the story—the physical existence in which their bodies are living. The transition is automatic, as unconscious as highway driving. Often readers might cease to register where they are or what they are doing for minutes at a time. In this peculiar condition, a misspoken word, or a loud noise from outside the room, or an inquiry from a flight attendant as to whether one might like to try some more red wine, can be as harshly jarring as when we are abruptly awakened from our sleep.

Storytelling is thus not simply inscribing the storyteller's signals upon the blank sheet of the listeners' thinking. Readers cannot shut off their consciousness and turn on the story at will. Their minds are incapable of being so silent or submissive. Their own threshold consciousness continues, but it is pushed into the background by the more insistent and seductive suggestions of the storyteller.

At times, notes Birkerts, the readers find the two voices—their own and the storyteller's—in dissonant conversation. When the story flags, for whatever reason, the self-murmurings of the reader's mind rush in to fill the void.

Surely, I think, the same phenomenon must be occurring in oral storytelling: I as storyteller might be rambling on about Zambia, while the listener is thinking about her rapidly filling in-box. If Zambia becomes too indistinct, she might be unable to resist the temptation to get back to her desk and begin sifting through the incoming deluge of messages that inevitably will have to be dealt with.

When fully engaged, Birkerts argues, the readers' minds work in concert with the storyteller to focus entirely on generating the virtual world of the story. As a result of the cooperative enterprise, the readers' consciousness presides over the movements in a world that comes into view and vanishes. It is a virtual world in which time is structured and foreshortened, compared to the struggle and chaos of the readers' own days. In this condition of following a story, the readers can even feel a sense of connectedness that is more direct and vivid than their actual lived reality. From inside an absorbing story, the readers can feel an agility and limberness, a sense of being for once in accord with time, real time, deep time, an environment where events resonate and have meaning. They have a feeling that the whole of their lives—past as well as future—is somehow available to them both as a lived-through experience and as an object of contemplation. Despite their isolation as separate individuals, a story generates a sense that they are nevertheless connected. Inside a story, the readers' lives appear, at least momentarily, as through a lens that makes sense, as though the hazy fragments of experience for once come suddenly into focus. In following a story, they remap their own lives in relation to the universe. This remapping not only determines and informs the actions of the characters in the story, but also creates new coordinates for grasping the reality of the readers' own existence.

Thus, over and above the transmittal of linguistic signals, the audience's perspective on the rest of the world has the tendency, while it is following the story, to become altered. For the duration of the story, and sometimes beyond, the audience's participation in this imaginary world can change their perceived relation to all other things. The change has as much to do with the process of the storytelling as with the particular story being told.

～

I stop reading Birkerts for another mouthful of wine. I am forced to admit that he has given me a compelling delineation of what is occurring in storytelling. The contrast with abstract analysis is stark. Abstract thinking is radically different and detached. The listener stands back and apart, as if viewing the scene through a window, a passive observer of the language. When it comes to Aristotle's splendid generalizations, such as, "All men are mortal," we can slide over the gleaming smoothness of such generalities from one end to the other without stopping. A concept such as "all men" has no place to get a handle on it, or a feel for its meaning. Taken even further, in the pure form of abstract thinking—mathematics—the equation

$$y = x + a$$

comes to us with no unexpected associations, no fuzzy allusions to prior experiences, no hints of unexpected linkages, no excess mental baggage. Such generalities demand no imaginative collaboration from the listeners in conjuring up a virtual world in envisaged time and space. The speaker transmits a signal, and the listeners inscribe it on the blank screens of their minds for analysis, calculation, and evaluation. The characters in mathematical or general propositions—$x$ or $y$

or *a*—have no personalities, no attitudes, no quirks. They lack the habits or idiosyncrasies that might give them the interest of anything living.

The listeners' minds might be active when they handle mathematics and abstractions, but they are active in a different fashion from their participation in a narrative. In doing so, they are not beguiled into adding their own experience or background. On the contrary, they are more or less obliged to put out of their minds anything other than the signal that the speaker is transmitting. They are invited to keep at bay their own imaginations, their own experiences, their own personal backgrounds—anything, in fact, that might be distracting, anything that would interfere with the exactitude of the language that is being transmitted. In this respect, the lived experience of participating in abstract thinking is fundamentally different in character from that of following a story, where the active participation and contributions of the listener are well-nigh essential if the storytelling is to be effective.[6]

In abstract thinking, listeners—apart perhaps from professional mathematicians—are not transported to any magic land of generalities, a conceptual elsewhere that we can recognize, or in which listeners can feel much comfort. The world of abstraction remains an uninhabited and uninviting place. No cold winds blow there. No sun shines into the lives of *x* or *y* or *a*. It is a world without weather, or even air, and it is empty of any purpose. This universe is immaculately crisp and clean and neat, full of sharp edges and straight lines, a world that is inert and, in the end, dead.

By contrast, when I am telling a story about an idea I am trying to communicate—it happens in my case to be an idea of sharing knowledge, but it might be on any number of topics—there is some-

---

[6] If one accepts that metaphors permeate language, and that metaphors are miniature stories, then the distinction between abstract language and narrative is not a sharp distinction: George Lakoff, The Contemporary Theory of Metaphor, in *Metaphor and Thought*, 2nd ed., edited by Andrew Ortony. Cambridge, U.K., and New York: Cambridge University Press, 1993.

where, a notional place, for the listeners to visit on their virtual journey. For example, when I tell listeners about a health worker in Zambia who logged on to a Web site in Atlanta on the other side of the globe and got the answer to a question on how to treat malaria, I am implicitly inviting the listener to live the story with me, to follow the experience of the health worker, to relive the momentary professional dread of being asked a centrally important question and not having an adequate answer, as well as the imminent triumph that derives from finding it within minutes on the World Wide Web. It is a brief experience, but nevertheless—if the listener understands the context—a living experience. For anyone who has been in an out-of-the-way place and baffled for lack of the answer to an urgent and important problem, the experience of listening to such a story can be vivid enough to spark the mind into having further important thoughts that could lead to meaning, generate understanding, give impetus to the will, and eventually catalyze action.

As the flight toward London continues, I take from my leather briefcase a file that I have brought on the flight and look at the abstract definition of knowledge management that I noted from one of the world's best Web sites:

> *Knowledge Management caters to the critical issues of organizational adaptation, survival, and competence in face of increasingly discontinuous change. Essentially, it embodies organizational processes that seek synergistic combination of data and information processing capacity of information technologies, and the creative and innovative capacity of human beings.*[7]

Impeccably comprehensive, and profound in its implications, the definition has only one problem: it is unintelligible except to someone who already understands the subject. The definition is not wrong. It is rather that one would have to know the topic in depth before one could realize why the definition might be right. Even then, an experi-

---

[7] The Biz Tech Network: *www.brint.com*

enced practitioner needs a considerable mental effort just to comprehend it. As an answer to the question as to what is knowledge management, it could appear to confirm the cynic's worst suspicions that the concept of knowledge management is hopelessly complex and confused, and in the end irrelevant.

By contrast, I can see how little in the way of mental energy the story of the health worker in Zambia needs:

> *In June 1995, a health worker in Kamana, Zambia, logged on to the CDC Web site in Atlanta and got the answer to a question on how to treat malaria.*

The explicit story is simple and accessible. If the listener understands the context of what it is like to be a health worker in the outback of a country like Zambia and is able to extrapolate from the anecdote this experience across other organizations and other contexts, then the gist of knowledge management can be transmitted more rapidly and efficiently than in grappling with a logically accurate, abstract definition. This re-creation of the idea of knowledge management by analogy from a story can happen if the story stimulates the listeners to think actively about the implications: "Imagine if other organizations had made their expertise available in the same way as the Centers for Disease Control—how many more clients and partners they might reach!" When the story does its job, the listeners' minds race ahead, to imagine the further implications of elaborating the same idea in other contexts, better and more intimately known to the listeners. In this way, through extrapolation from the anecdote, the re-creation of the idea of knowledge management can be successfully brought to birth, with the concept of it planted in listeners' minds, not as a vague abstract inert thing, but an idea that is pulsing, kicking, breathing, exciting—and alive.

‹〜

Sven Birkerts stresses that the process of following a story is easy and almost automatic. People enjoy it and are willing to pay money to be so entertained. By contrast, explanations force us into an abstract way of thinking, which our minds tend to find tiring. Relatively few people are willing pay money to take lessons in mathematics or symbolic logic solely for the sake of entertainment.

Surely this difference has something to do with why a story can generate positive attitudes to change, when clear instructions don't.

I think back to a not-too-previous weekend when I had gone with my young daughter to a local toy store. She had selected a toy with which I had agreed to indulge her; I paid for it, and then we went to collect it at the pickup station. To my dismay, when we came to get the item, I saw that the box in which it was packed was flat and did not at all resemble what my daughter and I had seen on display. The sales clerk reassured me that there was no mistake: the box contained the correct item that we had seen. It was simply that the toy was shipped disassembled. My heart sank.

"It's very easy," she said with a bright smile. "Only a few simple steps needed to put it together. No sweat."

But I was already sweating. Recollections of earlier struggles with self-help furniture and kits for appliances that needed to be assembled were flooding through my mind. These were not pleasant memories. "Place Rod A in Slot F and secure with Screw P in Hole X." It wasn't that the job was impossible, or even that the instructions were not technically impeccable. In each case, I eventually located Rod A, after discerning the difference between it and Rods B and C, along with Slot F, Screw P, and Hole X, and thus ultimately succeeded in assembling the item in accordance with the manufacturer's instructions.

But it wasn't an enjoyable experience. In each case, I had eventually done everything requested and had in due course met with success. But I felt little pleasure or sense of accomplishment in having completed the task. Rather, I felt tired, worn out, put upon. There was no room for error. In fact, the slightest deviation from the instructions generally caused the whole installation to fail. Any false step, or even the right step in the wrong sequence, required me to go backwards, undo the work that I had already done, and start afresh. Any innovation that I might contribute almost inevitably led to disaster, since in this scheme of things, innovation was equivalent to error. In fact, there was no room for me to add anything. The result was that I had the feeling of being used. If someone were to propose that I assemble another such item—just for fun—I knew that my response would be very negative. The last thing I would want to do then would be to follow another rigid set of instructions. I would have a drink, go outside, walk the dog, do some chores—anything, except to follow another set of instructions.

Now it dawns on me. Surely I am not alone in having these feelings toward following a sequence of detailed instructions! Many others must feel as I do. Even if such feelings were not innate or even universal, they must be quite widespread.

Moreover, I note that we are considering here not a *poor* explanation of how to do something, but instead a virtually perfect explanation—edited, vetted, checked for error, replete with sketches to illustrate the text. Yet despite its perfection, it generates a feeling of frustration, a feeling of being imposed upon.

By comparison with step-by-step explanations, I can follow stories with pleasure and with no effort at all. The process happens instantly, often without conscious effort. I can go on doing it all day and feel refreshed at the end of it. Like many people, I find the practice of participating in storytelling natural, enjoyable, and relaxing. Most important, it is energizing. Filling in the gaps in a story generates, rather than depletes, energy. I have more energy at the end than when I begin.

⤚

As I look back on the stories that I have told, I realize that the Zambia story has left a lot unsaid about how the health worker in Kamana happened to be looking for a solution through a computer on the Web, or how CDC happened to have material on the very question to which the health worker was looking for an answer, or what else was going on in Kamana at the time. I omitted to say anything about these aspects, but it didn't seem to matter. The listeners imagined what was in the gaps. The listeners had been willing to join hands with me as the storyteller and fill in the missing links of a story to the extent necessary.

This willingness was a remarkably helpful attribute of storytelling. In some instances, when I had been trying to explain knowledge management, I would simply not have known enough to convey how it would work out in practice. I could not have spelled out the interconnections even if I had tried, in terms of providing the complete explanation of how the equivalent of Rod A in knowledge management fitted into the equivalent of Slot F. Even if I had attempted it, I would have gotten a lot wrong. Moreover, the listeners wouldn't have wanted it, and they couldn't have absorbed it even if it was given. It would have been a mistake to try to convey static information, when I was in fact dealing with a dynamic, shifting approach.

When I told a story, once the listeners had taken on board the overall gestalt of sharing knowledge from the story, they could later go on to provide the missing links on their own. They could figure out for themselves that we would need something like Rod A, and that there must be somewhere to put it, something along the lines of Slot F— and so they could improvise that, too.

Once the listeners had gotten the basic idea of knowledge sharing, they could think through for themselves that we would need something like a community of practice, and it would have to be located somewhere in the organization, and so they could improvise that, too, with their colleagues. In the process, they became co-creators of the design of the knowledge-sharing program.

In narrative, there is thus an implicit invitation to the listeners to fill in the missing links in the story. If the listeners accept the invitation, they are thus inside the story, projecting themselves into the situation, living the predicament of the protagonist, feeling what he or she was feeling, experiencing the same hopes and fears. In such a lived-in experience, it is not difficult for the participants to visualize the missing links. In fact, they will find it difficult to resist adding necessary patterns and linkages to the narrative.

This process of having the listeners fill in the missing links helps explain another puzzle—why stories can capture and regenerate dynamically evolving concepts. Thus, while the idea of knowledge sharing has kept steadily evolving—from collections of knowledge, to collections and connections, to communities of practice, to partnerships—and the abstract description of the program has had to be steadily updated and changed to reflect the shifting reality, the stories don't seem to need updating. Even as the content of the knowledge-sharing program has changed, the explicit stories have stayed the same. It is the listeners' interpretation of them that changes. It is as if the stories have spare DNA built into them that can be adapted by the listeners to a variety of new situations. The meaning is not in the story itself, but rather in the meaning that the listeners create out of the story, linked to their new context. As the change idea changes, the additional meaning brought by the listeners attach to the previously unnoticed feature of the context—the unused DNA—so as to create an updated meaning.

As I review the stories that I have used in the past few years, they all still look good. Hidden even from me as the unwitting storyteller are all of the elements of my future meanings. I have transmitted meaning without realizing it.

꙰

Now, as I look around the airplane cabin, I can see that the only passenger light still illuminated is mine, and it is only the flight attendants and I who are not trying to sleep. So I finally close my eyes, paying silent tribute to Sven Birkerts and Virginia Woolf for having spurred me on this journey.

As I begin to doze, I can dimly recognize that abstract thinking works by similes, where the point of comparison is constrained to a certain dimension or effect. The narrative model, by contrast, works by metaphor, with potentially unlimited points of comparison, including all sorts of potential hidden connections that might emerge later, when the context changes. In a new telling, the context generates a new set of spectacles in which we live the story anew.

Abstract thinking mimics the physical world in a limited fashion and then looks at the resulting predictions. In the narrative mode of thinking, the participants visualize and live the story in the mind's eye, and so experience the story as if they are living inside it. From within the story, they can get a feel for multiple aspects of the situation, immerse themselves in it, and get a fresh sense of perspective. The coordinates of one story, deeply felt, enable the listener to understand another.

The abstract way of thinking leaves us as perpetual spectators, self-conscious and external—turning us into voyeurs who observe the world as though through an impermeable glass screen. The universe of verifiable truth to which this type of thinking aspires can produce generalizations that are useful, but that also turn out to be inert.

By contrast, the narrative way of thinking is internal and immersive and self-forgetting and attached to the full richness of tacit understanding. Through a story, life invites us to come inside as a participant.

# FIVE

# A Tale of Two Stories

*The explicit meanings of the actual words ride on the surface of this depth like waves on the surface of the sea.*

David Abram, *The Spell of the Sensuous*[1]

*When we dream alone, it is only a dream. When we dream together, it is no longer a dream but the beginning of reality.*

Brazilian proverb

Around me on the transatlantic flight coming into London, aching bodies and stiff limbs slowly stir and stretch and come to premature morning life. I have dozed for what is no more than a few moments, but my mind is flying in all directions.

The aircraft descends through the clouds to set down on a wet runway. From the ground, the sky has a tint of zinc, and memories of England's green and pleasant land are quickly banished by the dank reality of the windy, wet, cold weather. An interminable taxi ride through a massive London traffic jam takes me through the maze of narrow throatlike roads and eventually deposits me in a quixotic hotel, in which the corridors have to be negotiated rather than walked through. My hotel room is a strange shape, practically a miniature labyrinth, where the bathroom fixtures hardly work. It is the sort of

---

[1] David Abram. *The Spell of the Sensuous: Perception and Language in a More-than-Human World.* New York: Pantheon Books, 1997.

building that in New York would have been demolished decades ago, but in London might still be flourishing a hundred years hence.

After a quick wash and shave, I descend to the underground facility where the international business conference is being held. As usual at such affairs, the participants come from many different companies and countries and backgrounds, but this time, the mood coalesces into a common tone. On this occasion, instead of the arrogance frequently exuded by conference speakers who profess to know it all and talk of stunning successes that they could not possibly have enjoyed, the mood here is an attractive one of modesty and questioning and searching. The speakers are openly pondering the quandaries in which they find themselves.

My presentation is to take place the next day, and so I have the luxury of listening to the ebb and flow of discussion.

My assigned topic is the emerging knowledge economy. But when I listen to what people are saying, I find that there is a much greater interest and concern and puzzlement about a different subject—namely, how to convey the complex and still-exotic concept of knowledge management to somewhat baffled leaderships back at their respective headquarters. The participants have been trying out abstract explanations and reasons, but they seem to have been experiencing universal difficulty in getting anyone to listen.

A young English woman tells of her plucky but ultimately unsuccessful attempts to get her bank to understand knowledge management. An energetic chemist discusses his struggle to get shared agreement for a honeycomb structure of a new chemical company. A gentleman from a record company tells about his efforts to reflect more fully what went into a decision, the reasons behind the decision, the feelings at the time, what else the decision maker would like to have known, and links to other documents. A Scandinavian lady worries about how she is going to transfer tacit knowledge. An engineer from an oil company discusses its structure in terms of a sunflower with skills at its center, and petals that suggest learning, recognition, assessment, and progression. Everyone recognizes the immense impediments that social barriers and organizational culture represent. Everywhere it is a question of selling the concept, with many experiments and small-scale efforts well under way, but everyone is having difficulty in getting full institutional buy-in.

As I listen to this discussion, I am all the while developing and rearranging my presentation to plug into the ebb and flow. I sense that these are people who want to learn. By their own accounts, they are all "going by the book." The methods that they are following to sell the concept are those that are widespread in the most admired organizations of our time, as well as those recommended in textbooks. Examples of such thinking are evident everywhere. One well-known example is in *Leading Change* by John Kotter, as encapsulated by the following passage:

> *Imagine the following. Three groups of ten individuals are in a park at lunchtime with a rainstorm threatening.*
>
> *In the first group, someone says, "Get and up and follow me." When he starts walking and only a few others join in, he yells to those still seated, "Up, I said and NOW."*
>
> *In the second group, someone says: "We're going to have to move. Here's the plan. Each of us stands up and marches in the direction of the apple tree. Please stay at least two feet away from other group members and do not run. Do not leave any personal belongings on the ground here and be sure to stop at the base of the tree. When we are all there. . . . "*
>
> *In the third group, someone tells the others: "It's going to rain in a few minutes. Why don't we go over there and sit under that huge apple tree. We'll stay dry, and we can have fresh apples for lunch."*[2]

In his book, Kotter argues that the first two approaches, which he calls authoritarian decree and micro-management, will be ineffective. "Only the third approach," says Kotter, "has the potential to break

---

[2] John Kotter, *Leading Change.* Boston: Harvard Business School Press, 1996, p. 69.

through all the forces that support the status quo and to encourage the kind of dramatic shifts found in successful transformations."[3]

It is this third approach that the participants at the London conference are generally following, yet finding it just as unproductive as the first two.

And yet it isn't too hard to see what is going to happen if one follows this approach, even in the apple tree example. In that case, people will look at the speaker and then at the rain clouds and say—or think—What makes you so sure it's going to rain? In any event, what's the rush? Why not wait and see whether it really does rain? If it rains, we'll move, but if not, why bother? We are having fun, lunching and discussing. If you want to go and pick apples, that's fine, so why don't you go? But for those of us who don't, why don't we just go on sitting here, having our lunch and having a good time? And right now someone is telling an interesting story and I want to listen to that. . . .

Underlying the illusion that providing reasons leads to immediate agreement is a set of assumptions about communicating complex ideas that is as obsolete as it is rotten.

Thus, the conference participants have found that human communication does not proceed like clockwork. In Kotter's model, there is someone—it isn't clear who—who has the idea of "moving the group to the apple tree." In the model, things work like clockwork. Suggest the idea. Give the reason. People listen. People do what you say. In more difficult economic times, when people were frightened that losing their jobs meant losing their future and supervisors had coercive power over employees, the approach might have worked to a certain extent. Now that employees no longer expect lifetime employment with one firm, such approaches and assumptions are likely to send the best employees scouring job opportunities elsewhere. The suggestion that people listen to the idea, and act on it simply because

---

3 Kotter, p. 70.

someone proposes a reason for implementing it, is contrary to experience and common sense. People simply don't react this way.

Nor does human communication proceed on the basis of pure reason.

As the participants in the London conference have found, the instigator of change is not generally facing an inherently receptive audience. Even in a social setting, when someone proposes to a group that is already having a good time at lunch to move somewhere else at once, the reaction cannot be expected to be receptive unless the proposer has done something to get the group into a receptive mood. In the apple tree example, an abrupt proposal that the group move—without more than a reason—is virtually certain to be met with skepticism, unless the reason happens to mesh with whatever the group is currently discussing and feeling. If, for instance, the group is bored and is looking for a change, the proposal might work, but then practically by accident, and not for the reason put forward by the person proposing it. If, on the other hand, the group is having a good time, the mere proffer of a reason that seems good to the speaker won't necessarily meet the group's needs. The instigator of change cannot expect instant receptiveness to reason, if he makes a specific change proposal that the group isn't expecting and that doesn't mesh with its ongoing dynamic.

In fact, also built into the approach is the defunct assumption that success for a group is doing what one person wants. Success in getting people to move has to involve an openness to submitting the idea itself (moving to the apple tree) to scrutiny as to whether it is good or bad, or whether it suits the group's dynamic, or whether it will lead the group where it wants to be. Only if the group ends up owning the idea as its own, not just following the idea of the proposer, is it likely to be energetically implemented.

In order to succeed in getting the group to see it as their own, there has to be a deeper understanding. Why is this group of people there anyway? What is their objective? Perhaps to have a pleasant lunch together. Are abrupt moves at the behest of one person likely to be compatible with this? Only if the group can see that making a move would be more fun than sitting there and talking and listening to other people and waiting for the rain to come, and then if necessary, picking up one's things as the first drops come down and making a dash for it and arriving breathless and slightly damp but energized and laughing and none the worse for the moisture. If in fact the group can't see that making the move now will be more fun than that, then the group will—without more—be unwilling to move at once. Unless the instigator of change can present the idea in a way that makes it seem like more fun, it will fizzle. And further: what is wrong with the group staying where they are? If the group is having more fun just staying there, why not let them be? Unless success is defined as "getting you to do what I want," the group might well be right not to move.

It is thus hard to get people to accept predetermined ideas, or well-articulated plans that have been generated by someone else. It will be easy for a disappointed instigator of change to interpret the lack of responsiveness as resistance. One might even begin to suspect that people innately resist change. But the resistance experienced from others is not to change itself, but rather to the particular process of change that believes in imposition rather than co-creation of what needs to be done.[4]

So if we want the group to move, we have to spark a different kind of process, a process that will enable the group to see that moving to the apple tree is an idea that they create and own, and will seem like more fun than staying where they are.

Thus, if the group believes that a couple of celebrities are hiding in the apple tree, it will be difficult to stop them from going there to have a look. Or if we could get a discussion going on the superior properties of apple trees in affording protection against the rain versus

4 Margaret Wheatley and Myron Kellner-Rogers, *A Simpler Way*. San Francisco: Berrett-Koehler Publishers, 1996, p. 99.

other kinds of trees, one might be able to spark their curiosity so that when the rain came they would in fact move to try it out. Or if there is a discussion about the superior nutritional value of the particular brand of apple of that tree, the group might start to think about eating apples, and then when the rain comes, move. Or if we can't spark any such process, and get this idea of moving to the apple tree to emerge from the group, then we might have to reconsider whether moving to the apple tree now is a good idea for this group anyway.

Why can't people in organizations see the fundamental flaws in the underlying assumptions? If we peel the conceptual onion one more layer, we can see that the mode of conduct being advocated is implicitly treating people as things to be manipulated. The course of conduct recommended by Kotter implies treating people as if one does not trust their judgment to come to a conclusion as to what to do, or drawing on their creativity to come up with perhaps even better ideas. Instead, the outcome, and in effect the criterion for success, has already been predetermined by the speaker (move to the apple tree) and the only question is how to get the group to do what the speaker has predetermined.

In a real-life social context with our friends, we do not act in the way that Kotter recommends in his apple tree example. In a social context, with our friends, we typically treat other people as people, not as things to be manipulated. (Or if we don't, we end up not so much with friends, as with business acquaintances who will also be trying to use us for their own purposes.)

But somehow in organizations, we have slid into the practice of treating people as things, and now business schools are even implicitly recommending it as good practice. The result is that trust breaks down, and the ability of organizations to enlist the cooperation of their employees is collapsing, precisely at the moment, in the knowledge economy, when organizations are increasingly dependent on enlisting that support.

Why does someone as intelligent and well-informed as Kotter fall into the trap of treating people as things? If we unpeel his conceptual onion by one final layer, we find that lying at the center is fear. If people, whether employees in organizations or people having lunch under an apple tree, are treated as people, rather than as things, then there is a risk that they might not accept the idea that we have come to propose to them, namely, move to the apple tree—or accept knowledge management, or whatever. This risk creates fear. We become frightened that the people might decide that it is not a good idea. Or they might come up with a different and better idea, which will be their idea, not ours. Instead of relaxing, and learning to accept these possibilities as good potential outcomes to have at hand, and enjoying the fruits of the creativity of the group, fear of loss of control is prevalent, and so modes of behaving and talking evolve—and in Kotter's case are recommended—that are generally ineffective.

This is the typical thinking about organizational change at the end of the late twentieth century, a world in which fear lies at the very center.[5]

Out of fear, managers are relentlessly grinding along with their clockwork models, their vertical hierarchies, their treatment of people as things to be programmed and manipulated. The ineffectiveness of it all is exacerbated by the managers' subliminal awareness that the underlying assumptions are passé. Hence the wondering as to why they are unable to lead change, and why the innumerable books on leading change don't seem to help them.

⌐

---

[5] W. Edwards Deming was right about the need to drive out fear, although he was writing many years earlier and he didn't quite get to the reasons why the fear was there in the first place. The fear is not coming alone from the employees. The fear starts at the very top. See W. Edwards Deming, *Out of the Crisis*. Cambridge, MA: Massachusetts Institute of Technology, Center for Advanced Engineering Study, 1986.

That evening, I am invited by a participant for a drink. The initial conversation is stiff, until my host admits—implausibly, given his patrician demeanor—a strong liking for the singing group the Spice Girls. This prompts an unfettered conversation that meanders in various directions including the death of Princess Diana and the accomplishments of Nelson Mandela, before finally making its way back to the day's proceedings.

"What did you think of the discussion today?" he inquires.

"Everyone is struggling," I say. "Including us."

"No, I think you're really on a roll."

"We're still at the beginning."

"You know I've been visiting your organization for more than fifteen years. I had come to the conclusion that the place would never change. But I don't say that any more. Things are really on the move. The difference is visible."

"We've got a long way to go."

"But look how far you've come."

Wishing to change the subject, I say: "What do you think they want to hear tomorrow?"

"You should tell them what you did and how you did it."

"That's not my topic," I say. "I'm meant to be talking about the twenty-first century knowledge economy."

"Stick to what you did. It will be a lot more interesting."

The conversation moves on, but I think he has a point. The question that will be on everyone's lips that night in the bars and restaurants of Kensington is how to sell a concept and transfer tacit understanding.

But what should I present? That civilization is resting on a footing of unspoken fear? That individuals, in putting forward their ideas in abstract generalities, are unwittingly going into control modes of interaction in order to fend off inklings of their mounting internal self-doubt? Even if I fire off such a broadside, and the audience buys it, will it be productive, or will it immobilize them from further action?

Fear is the darkest part of our beings. It is the last thing that people are willing to reveal. A business conference is premised on optimism, performance, presentation, and individual success, not recognition of inner terror.

That the collection of thinking individuals gathered in the underground conference room in London will accept such wild ideas is as implausible as expecting that my own organization would have accepted a straightforward and rational argument in favor of knowledge management.

I can see that if I recommend directly to the London participants that they abandon their current way of acting and thinking, they will probably react badly. It will set up an adversarial relationship with a less-than-happy ending.

And so, I opt instead to let the medium reflect the message. My host is right. I will not tell them what to do, or even suggest that what they are doing is wrong. Instead, I will simply tell them my story. I will say what I have done and how I did it, and why I think it has been successful. I will let the listeners draw their own conclusions about the implications for their own situation.

Even so, I am uneasy. The idea that the blurry workings of the listeners' subthreshold murmurings might be more effective in catalyzing understanding and action than direct and explicit instructions is still counterintuitive to me, despite my recent experience. I am still in the thrall of what I have been taught from a young age concerning the overriding advantages of directness and clarity. My carefully trained intellectual reflexes still cry out: why not spell out the message directly? Why go to the trouble and difficulty of trying to elicit the listeners' thinking indirectly, when it will be so much simpler if I come straight out in an abstract directive. Why not hit the listeners between the eyes instead of sidling up on them with an indirect and ambiguous message, as if whispering in their ears?

Nevertheless, I control these urges and decide that, instead of recommending storytelling directly, I will tell them my story of storytelling.

～

It is late at night in my hotel room in London and I start preparing the requisite slides, which will tell the audience of my own problems in getting anyone to listen. I explain how I have found charts generally ineffective. I have tried prose but no one reads it. Dialogue with individuals one-on-one is fine, but it takes too long to get to all of the ten thousand people in our organization. What then? I tell them how I told the story of Zambia.

> In June 1995, a health worker in Kamana, Zambia, logged on to the CDC Web site in Atlanta and got the answer to a question on how to treat malaria.

Twenty-nine words. A mere 200 bytes. Why did so many people listen? Why did it have such an apparently magical impact?

I will say that there is no such thing as magic, no matter how convincing the magician might be on stage. At a magic show, the audience has the illusion of magic occurring, because their attention is pointed in one direction, so that they don't see what the magician is doing somewhere else. The magician's assistant is already hidden in the haunted house, the rabbit is already in the hat, the eggs are already up the magician's sleeve.

A magician, wishing to preserve the magic, never explains how the trick was done and so preserves the mystification, which is part of the pleasure of magic. It seems unreal. But my object is to enlighten, rather than to mystify, and so I will tell the conference how I think the apparent magic is happening.

The previous speakers at the London conference have all been assuming that communication entails a communicator who has a lot of explicit information to communicate, and that somehow in the process of communication this information has to be transmitted to the minds of the listeners. What they have been finding is that this transfer simply isn't physically possible. There is too much information to transmit. There isn't enough time to transmit it, let alone enough patience on the part of listeners. What is to be done?

The first key to understanding the problem is to stop seeing communication as information transfer, where one person has a huge mental bin of information in his or her mind that is transmitted to the minds of the listeners. Instead we are dealing with an interaction in which the listeners already have huge mental bins of information of their own. If we start trying to transfer huge mental bins of information over to them, there is never enough time to complete the transfer. Even if there was, there would be a massive problem for the listeners not only as to where to put all this new information in their minds—where would the mind's librarian file it?—but also how to reconcile it with the information and perceptions and attitudes that they already have.

Instead we need to realize not only that the listeners already have huge mental bins of implicit or tacit information at their disposal, but also that the implicit or tacit information is not something that needs to be moved out to make room for the new, but rather something that can be catalyzed into a new pattern of understanding reality. If we can draw on the large volumes of existing implicit information, then there is no need for a huge information transfer. The listeners already have most of the information they need. We need to stop seeing the existing information in their minds as a problem, and start seeing it as a potential solution.

This is where the springboard story comes in. A tiny story—29 words or 200 bytes—is less a vehicle for communication of large amounts of information and more a tiny fuse that ignites a new story in the listeners' minds, which establishes new connections and patterns in the listeners' existing information, attitudes, and perceptions.

The new story helps rearrange the huge amount of tacit knowledge already with the listeners so that they can understand the connections between things in a different sense. The listeners generate a new story.

〜

Communicating a complex message to an audience with strong views of its own can be likened to rowing a boat across a fast-moving river. If we aim the boat precisely toward the point to which we want to arrive, on the opposite shore, we can be sure that we will not arrive where we want to go, and instead, we will arrive somewhat further down river. If we want to arrive at a certain point, we need to ascertain in which direction the river is flowing and how fast, and then point the boat somewhat upstream, so that the combination of our initial aim and the impact of the flow of the river will take us to our destination. We might make many course corrections while making the crossing so that our estimates of the interaction between the speed of our rowing and the speed of the river can be calibrated in real time.

If we are focusing solely on the message we are trying to send, we will see the speed and force of the intervening river—the inputs from the listeners—as regrettable interference or distortion, something unfortunate that has to be minimized or eliminated, if at all possible. We will use scientific or abstract communications that keep the listener's inputs at bay. On the other hand, if we are taking advantage of a story, and its accompanying springboard effect, the inputs from the listeners enter the picture as energy-generating enhancements that help to get us to our intended destination.

Thus, when we want to cross the river of communication, we anticipate the speed and force of the river—the inputs from the listeners—and use these inputs as a positive element to help get us to our destination. In the physical instance, we do this instinctively: we don't aim the boat directly where we want to go. We aim it upstream, allowing for the force of the river.

In conversation one-on-one, we intuitively understand this phenomenon, in part because we get instantaneous negative feedback if we barge into a dialogue on the assumption that our original input will be registered by our listeners and accepted without question or distortion, or if we start telling people how to think about a subject, without taking the time to find out what is going on in their own minds. Thus, we learn from a young age that in conversation we often cannot go in a straight line from A to B: we first have to get into an interactive mode with the listener and work our way step-by-step toward the goal.

Generally, as a result of our formal training, most of us had tended to operate in our organizational behavior in the directly opposite fashion. The focus of our attention is often solely on the message being sent, and we pay little or no attention to inputs from the listener. It should hardly be a surprise to us when the end result of the communication is very different from what we intend.

If we think about the inputs from listeners as a variable at all, it is usually to reassure ourselves, like Kotter, either that the inputs from listeners will be insignificant or that the listeners will be sympathetic to our cause and add positive value. Unfortunately, when it comes to proposing major change in organization, these assumptions rarely correspond to the actual situation.

⌒

It is now past midnight as I look over the slides that I have prepared for the presentation the next day. They explain why an audience can project itself inside a story and become immersed in the flow of a narrative, so as to enhance understanding—one storyteller and one listener joined together in a common activity. But they don't give any clue why the stories that were generated closed the gap between idea and action so rapidly. Why do these stories lead, not merely to enhanced understanding, but also to quick forward action?

Despite the fabulous attributes of narrative, action is not often seen as a typical consequence of listening to a story. When we listen to stories, we may be entertained. We may be moved. We may laugh or we may cry. But we do not normally leap into action, let alone concerted action along with other listeners. So what is it in the stories I have been telling about knowledge sharing that has helped generate an action-oriented response?

The key seems to be that we are dealing not with one story, but two. Birkerts has pointed to the coexistence of the two voices that can occur in storytelling when the story is less than all-absorbing: the listeners hear the storyteller's telling of the story, but also hear their own silent voices within, as their minds ponder a variety of quite different thoughts. Birkerts considered—and deplored—the possibility that these two voices might be in *dissonant* conversation: the listener isn't listening! For Birkerts, who is looking at stories as entertainment, anything less than one hundred percent concentration on the story itself is a failure of storytelling.

And in storytelling for entertainment, something less than full absorption in the story can constitute a problem: the storyteller is rambling on about Zambia, while the listener is thinking about her rapidly filling inbox. Birkerts's wish as a lover of fictional narrative is to immerse himself fully in the magical world of the explicit narrative, and so leave behind his own drab reality. Any lack of attention to the storyteller's voice is seen by Birkerts as a regrettable shortcoming in the storyteller's art or the reader's willingness and ability to listen. Birkerts wants—even yearns—to have the more articulated, the more present language of the storyteller push his own subthreshold murmuring *totally* into the background, so that he, the reader, may be famously entertained.

And yet for the springboard storyteller, the storyteller whose purposes are not so much entertainment as to generate an action-oriented response in the listener, there is another interesting possibility, namely that the two voices of the listener and the storyteller can continue in parallel, but this time in *consonant* conversation. The storyteller might deliberately tell the story in such a way as to allow some mental space for the listeners to forge their own thoughts, with the explicit objective of having the listeners invent analogous stories of their own, in parallel to the storyteller's explicit story.

Here, the world of the explicit story is merely a springboard, a mere point of departure for new stories that the listeners will generate in their own minds, from their own environments, from their special contexts, from their own experience of problems. What is memorable for the listeners on such a journey will not be the moment of embarkation when they set out by way of the explicit story, but rather the virtual journey that they make of their accord to a destination that they themselves generate.

Thus, when listeners hear springboard stories in an organization aimed at achieving change—such as stories about the health worker in Zambia, or the task team in Chile or in Yemen—they are being reminded of the dilemma with which they are frequently confronted in their professional lives—that of being stuck in some remote country and being asked an urgent question to which they don't have the answer. The stories unfold for the listeners as a virtual experience through their projection on to the world of the protagonist in each of the stories. In the process, the listeners vicariously share the experience of the protagonist in unexpectedly finding an answer with the assistance of knowledge shared across organizational boundaries.

In such situations, I, as storyteller, am not particularly interested in informing the listeners about the specifics of the situations in Zambia or Chile or Yemen, or of the information systems, or of how the answers were delivered. What I am trying to do is to stimulate in the listeners' minds, at the same time, an analogous and future-oriented story based on the listeners' own experiences and contexts. I am eliciting a set of subthreshold murmurings that respond to the listeners' own problems. Most of the audience will not be familiar with the specifics of working in Zambia or Chile or Yemen, or even be thinking about these countries or their particular problems. Few of them would be working on the specific subject domains—health or education—in which the stories actually occurred. That doesn't matter.

What does matter is that many listeners are facing the dilemma of getting speedy answers to unexpected problems within tight deadlines. I as storyteller am thus stimulating the listeners to generate a stream of reflection along the following lines:

*Suppose I was part of such a network of like-minded and sharing professionals. Suppose that I had access to such a service. I could be more productive. I could help my clients and provide faster better services. I would have a solution. Suppose. . . .*

Once I have managed to stimulate these blurry subthreshold murmurings into existence, the seeds of the idea of knowledge sharing will have been successfully germinated. If the seeds of the idea can be nurtured with further elements to excite the listeners' imaginations, then the listeners can discover the idea of knowledge sharing in a way that makes it their own. What is more, the stories, because they are generated by the listeners themselves, will fit perfectly the listeners' own contexts and environment and problems. The vocabulary in which these subthreshold murmurings occur will be completely friendly and natural to the listeners, since it is they who created it.

Even more important, because the stories are the listeners' own, they are blessed with all the pride of ownership, and along with it, the will to implement. By leaving some space for the listeners to create their own stories, the storyteller can thus create the possibility for the listeners to become the sponsoring gods of their own stories—to become their own storytellers. They will remain in charge. They will not lose control. They will not have to submit to another's will. They will retain their own sense of identity and integrity, because they have generated the story themselves. In fact, the story will become part of their own evolving sense of identity. In this way, one can achieve mass customization of the message, by leaving space for the listeners themselves to create it.

～

Time has gone by and it is now well past midnight. My presentation is almost ready. Yet as I look over the slides, I find some in which I am giving the explicit directions to the audience for success. I realize that in order to generate a second implicit story, I have to take the final leap of faith in the listeners, and let them generate the story. I have to delete the explicit directions to the audience. The important thing is to create the springboard for the audience's thought. It is the story that the listeners invent for themselves as a result of the storyteller's story that is my real objective as storyteller. If I tell them what to conclude, then it will be my conclusion, not theirs. And we will be back in the adversarial mode of communication.

It takes a certain amount of confidence to drop the explicit directions. It is a level of confidence that I do not habitually possess. As I look over my slides now, I find myself tempted to keep the abstract conclusions and try, like some conceptual Napoleonic overlord, to lock in the view that I am intent on imposing on the world.

If I as the speaker am afraid that the listeners won't get the message, that only I know how to assemble the relevant concept of storytelling, that only I know how to select Rod A, and that only I know how to identify Slot F, then of course I will tell myself that I have to spell it out for them. In the process, I will risk getting them thoroughly confused, mixing up the whole with the parts, and causing them to forget what they have heard. To the extent that I am able to set this fear aside and trust the listeners to figure out how to make it work, having confidence that they will work out what is needed to make it function—to that extent, I can focus my efforts on communicating the big picture, the whole gestalt, and work out the details later.

Letting go of control sounds easy, but it is harder than it looks. It can easily be demonstrated by an old exercise from Japanese painting. Ancient painters used to practice putting dots on paper at random. This is surprisingly difficult. Even though I try to do it, what I do is always arranged in some order. I imagine to myself that I can let go of control in putting dots on paper, but in practice, I cannot. I find it impossible to arrange dots randomly.[6] So I have no illusions that it is easy to let go of control. On the contrary, try as I might, I find it creeping back into my actions and plans. Several millennia of effort by prior generations have bred it into me. It is like an insidious virus that assumes new forms, and disguises itself, to escape detection.

I have to force myself to relax and abandon control and tell a story that can spring the listeners to generate their own stories, which in some circumstances will have a strong enough gravitational pull, and provide a sufficiently compelling vision of the future, that a force field is generated, including the wish to become the different person. If this new identity is consistent with that of the storyteller, then the listeners have co-created the new vision of the future.

In retrospect, I can see that the first strong evidence of this phenomenon had followed the presentation, back in April 1996, when listeners came up to me after my presentation and kept asking me why the strategy I had presented was not already being implemented. "Why not?" they persisted. "What is the blockage?"[7]

The questions were framed as if knowledge sharing was their idea and not mine. They spoke to me as if they had discovered the idea of knowledge sharing and as if I was the one holding back progress. The idea had already entered their sense of identity.

Even more striking were my encounters with colleagues who had become leaders of communities of practice. I had known some of these people for years. Some of them had been natural leaders from the beginning. But in other cases, there was an apparent transformation in personality, as if they were becoming a different person. Before knowledge management, some had been scholarly researchers lost in their papers and reports and statistics. Others were busy practitioners who

---

6 Shunryu Suzuki, *Zen Mind, Beginner's Mind,* edited by Trudy Dixon. New York: Walker/Weatherhill, 1970, p. 32.

7 See Chapter 1.

were on the road most of the time and whose orientation totally focused on responding to individual clients. As these people began to assume leadership of their groups, it was striking to see the changes taking place in them. Now the researchers spoke with confidence and enthusiasm of practitioners. Now the practitioners had access to expertise. They had members around the world. They had vision. They had purpose. They had created their own stories. They talked to me as though their own identities had grown. Indeed, they looked to me as though they were several inches taller.

It is this effect that I am now trying to elicit in London. Now in the early hours of the morning in my tiny hotel room, I overcome the Napoleonic urge to tell the audience what to do and delete the explicit directives from the slides. I look at my watch and am shocked to see how late it is. I go to sleep for a few hours.

The next morning, I give my presentation to this group of people who have come to London to discuss knowledge management and who are engaged in the task of trying to persuade their top managerial teams to adopt it by giving abstract explanations and reasons in support thereof. They have been finding the going rather hard. They have been sensitized to the problem by the previous day's presentations. Now I tell them the story of my own experience in using stories to enable listeners to co-create their own analogous stories.

The indications of the success of the presentation are unequivocal. The standing ovation. The palpable flash of understanding in the room. The friendly tone of questions. The rush of participants after the session who want to hear more on how to use storytelling. The glow of admiration in the organizers' eyes.

It is one of those instants when one senses that all the parts of the universe are in harmony. More important, the whole conference suddenly gets the idea of storytelling with an instantaneous snap. The audience abruptly sees how storytelling could help solve its problems.

The participants all come from different organizations and back-grounds that I can only guess at, and they will all need to tell different stories to their respective managements. But I sense that the under-lying idea of using stories to convey complicated ideas is abruptly on their mental map.

# SIX

# Co-creating the Same Story

*In the act of narration, the narrators often end up telling a different story from that they imagined they were telling.*

Peter Brooks, *Reading for the Plot* [1]

**W**e learn more from our failures than from our successes. Success often depends heavily on serendipitous elements, on factors of which we are happily ignorant, or on the interweaving of causal threads in background patterns that we cannot even imagine. Face to face with our failures, we are obliged to recognize the minuscule contribution that we are able to add to a chaotic world, as well as to salute the influence of innumerable actors of whose existence we are often barely aware.

From the conference in London, I take a flight for Switzerland. On the journey, I am elated, as the conference presentation in London has gone better than I had any reason to expect. Mentally I have been traveling for so many months toward London, wondering what I was going to say on such a pompous topic as "the knowledge economy of the twenty-first century." Finally I have arrived. Yet the relish felt at having reached a destination is only temporary. The act of traveling has in a way been more satisfying than actually reaching the destina-

---

[1] Peter Brooks, *Reading for the Plot: Design and Intention in Narrative.* New York: A.A. Knopf, 1984, p. 262.

tion. The fact of arrival means getting ready for the next leg. The mere thought of a fresh challenge is enough to make me feel drained.

Now Switzerland—just ahead of me—is a very different situation. I have been invited to give a presentation to a group of managers and staff in a small public-sector agency. In principle, it is to be the same presentation as in London, but as I look ahead, I am already feeling tense. In itself, this is nothing unusual. Two days previously, I had felt the same way on coming into London. Each new audience is always a new challenge to tackle. Here in Bern, I have less of a sense of what I am getting into.

As it turns out, tonight, the entire European continent is in the throes of an enormous snowstorm, and Switzerland is in the middle of it. The flight from London to Bern is delayed, and when it does get under way, it is disturbed by violent turbulence. As the plane jars and bumps alarmingly, I tie my safety belt more tightly around my waist and try to remind myself that most planes end up landing safely at their destination. The reminder proves reliable. On arriving at the airstrip at Bern, I find that there are several inches of fresh powder on the ground, and more heavy flakes are floating down.

A fairytale bus ride from the airport through the Swiss countryside brings us to the center of the town, and I find myself booked into a grand and spacious hotel at the center of the city, cosseted by servants, amid lavish frescoes, tapestries, and antiques. The service is crisply Swiss and efficient.

In the morning, after a fitful night's sleep in a bedroom at least three times the size of the tiny labyrinth of the hotel room in London, I take a brief walk around the town that confirms that Bern has preserved more of its medieval aspect than other European towns. Glistening drifts of smooth white complete the traditional image of the scene. The architecture is a symbol of a kind of adherence to tradition and resistance to modernity. If ever a city could be said to be pretty, this is it.

The head of the agency that has invited me to come to Bern has also asked me to come to lunch. He is an affable man and is visibly pleased to have the pretext of a visiting speaker to invite his colleagues to an excellent local restaurant. The conversation seems to be mainly about local matters, of which I know nothing. A polite inquiry as to where I have come from gives me the opportunity to tell them about my presentation in London. The conversation quickly reverts to local issues, including a certain amount of jousting as to whether the fillets of Saint Pierre that we are eating come from the neighboring lake. From my imperfect understanding of the debate, I glean that my visit is something of a political football. Reading between the lines of a genial conversation, I can infer that there is no widespread enthusiasm for major change. I have been invited to come and make a presentation by certain elements who are basically pro-change, though they are still unclear as to its nature. My visit is part of their campaign for taking the agency into the future. As far as I can gather, the staff of the agency hold a variety of views—some hostile to change, some eager for change, some indifferent, some barely yet aware of the possibility. The guests at the lunch are polite but skeptical. I sense a general hesitancy about technology. In this alien terrain, with insufficient information of the conflicts and intersections of coalitions and individuals, it is difficult to get a grip on the overall geography.

After lunch, we go immediately to a meeting room to which some forty employees of the agency have been summoned. When I arrive, my surmise on the institutional politics of the situation is verified. I sense a myriad of crisscrossing agendas among the listeners. Amid some pockets of interest, I can feel both unease and puzzlement. Who am I? Why have I come? What part of the organization's plot do I fit into? Am I an irrelevant and momentary blip in an otherwise predictable world? Or am I a herald of a fundamentally different destiny?

As I try to think through how to adjust what I am going to say to the new situation, I realize that there is no time to reshape my presentation in any fundamental way, even though I can see where it is heading—a train wreck in the making.

A possible opportunity opens up when, on the first try, the projector doesn't register any connection, and there seems to be some incompatibility between it and my laptop. "Why don't we skip the slide presentation?" I venture, "And just go to discussion?"

"How do you mean?" my host inquires.

"We could improvise?" I say. "See what's on people's minds?"

My host insists, however, that it is essential to get the presentation, the real thing that I had just done at the conference in London. My own feelings are mixed. It will certainly be easier just to repeat the slides I had shown in London, with whose success I am still flushed. Yet in my own mind, I can sense the problems ahead. If the projector doesn't work, I won't need to decide. But suddenly, destiny intervenes. The technician has mended the projector and set up the connection. I can see on the screen my opening slide, a photo of a sunrise coming up behind a tree. My host says to get going.

There is no choice but to roll forward with the prepared presentation. All I can do is to modify what I say on the fly, and improvise as best I can on the spur of the moment to this disparate group of listeners about whom I know so little.

I go through the first part of my presentation on the new global economics of information that will inevitably transform the world economy, including that of Switzerland. The second part of my presentation covers the question of how organizations such as ours will cope with the new rules of the game. One of the ways will be by sharing knowledge. I tell them the story of sharing knowledge in Yemen, stressing that it isn't dependent on technology for its success. The third part of the presentation deals with what this might mean for an institution in Switzerland.

I finish and say that I'll be happy to take any questions.

There is silence. I cannot immediately decide whether it is the silence of delight, or the mortifying silence that occurs when a lecture has totally misfired.

Finally, a man's hand goes up slowly, and I invite him to speak. He says that he has never seen such a spectacular presentation. "Can you tell us more about the technology?" he says. "I mean, the technology of the presentation. What presentation program are you using? Where do you get those graphics?"

Right off the bat, we are heading off on a tangent. Here is a listener more impressed by the form of the presentation than the content, as if he has never seen before the wizardry of moving arrows, the wipes and folds that go from slide to slide, the luscious colors. The graphics, it seems, have been a distraction. I say that the software is nothing special. It is the same plain vanilla program that everybody uses. I insist that it is the idea of sharing know-how which is the substance of the presentation and to which I hope they will address their minds.

But one question on technology at once triggers another. "Do you think," says a young woman with thick spectacles, "that this technology is relevant to our situation? You're assuming everyone has computers, and is connected to the Web. But here in Bern, that's not what is going on. Most people don't use computers, and many people don't even like them. So I am worried that what you've presented here today is way ahead of what is possible for us in Switzerland. Maybe it would work in America, but I can't see how it could work here."

I reply again that I am not really talking about technology. "Knowledge sharing is about people, not machines. It is about connecting people who need to know with those who do know. The means by which they communicate is secondary. It can be face-to-face. It can be telephone. It doesn't have to be electronic messaging or the Web."

Another speaker follows up and says to look at the example of Yemen. "That kind of thing could never happen in Bern. People getting connected all around the world. Here in Bern," he says, "they simply don't have this fancy computer technology."

I say that this impression of people being connected by computers is an incorrect understanding of what happened in the Yemen example. On the contrary, the story of Yemen occurred, not through anything high-tech like the Web or electronic mail, but by the relatively old-fashioned technology of the telephone and the fax that is present and accessible in a country as little developed as Yemen, let alone Bern and the rest of the world. In any event, the world is moving fast, and it will not be too far into the future before the computer is as ubiquitous as these familiar instruments. And I insist yet again that this is not about technology. It is about sharing understanding between human beings.

There is a pause. I look around at the expressionless faces and realize that I am in the midst of the friends and abettors of Sven Birkerts. Many of them are perfectly in sync with his hostility to everything digital. I would have had more success with this group if I had read to them from *The Gutenberg Elegies:*

> *I worry not only that the world will become increasingly alien and inhospitable to me, but also that I will be gradually coerced into living against my natural grain, forced to adapt to a pace and a level of technological complexity that does not suit me, and driven to interact with others in certain prescribed ways.*[2]

Like Birkerts, these people are uneasy because the technology will impel them to have a certain kind of connectedness with their fellow men and women, using some new and unfamiliar tools, or risk being left behind. Even the thought of it is going against their natural grain.

"But surely," says another troubled listener, "this whole approach is more relevant for giant organizations like yours. We are just a tiny institution in a tiny country. We don't have your kind of funding. We can't afford to mobilize these kinds of resources."

I reply that sharing knowledge could be even more vital in a tiny organization because one can overcome the disadvantages of small size through connecting with other organizations, while retaining the advantages of agility.

I make the case, but the contentious questions continue, amid a few positive comments. But in general, I am dealing with the sullen-

---

[2] Sven Birkerts, *The Gutenberg Elegies: The Fate of Reading in an Electronic Age.* Boston: Faber and Faber, 1994, p. 28.

ness of skeptics, in place of the exultation I had just come across in London.

Finally, the session comes to end. The host thanks me, and we make the usual routine promises to follow up, to get together again.

$$\backsim$$

Later the same day, I go to the hotel bar, paneled in dark polished wood and white ceilings, where I am to meet a Swiss colleague. Our paths have crisscrossed over decades, and every several years we end up meeting like this, comparing our respective notes together over a glass of dark red wine.

After the usual exchange of pleasantries, during which we inquire after each other's wives and children, the conversation turns toward the presentation of that afternoon.

"You were terrific," he says.

"Nuts," I say. We have known each other for years, but he is still unaccustomed to my bluntness. "It was a mess."

He is polite enough to deny it and then looks at me in silence.

"We shouldn't be surprised," I say. "The presentation didn't connect. There was too much going on in that room. All sorts of agendas, everyone going off in all directions. The struggle for succession. The wish to stay the same. The urge to change. All going on at once. And all those questions about technology, as if technology had much to do with it. It's simply a different kind of discourse, individual to individual. These people don't think anything about talking on the telephone. They don't see that as anything different. And yet here they get all hung up on technology and the Web."

"You showed us what's going on in the world outside. That's at least what some of us wanted."

I say that I don't think that many people got it. The terror of technology has killed the gusto of the visionaries, so different from what happened in London.

"Perhaps," he says, "the Swiss are simply less demonstrative than the British."

"No, this isn't it," I say. "It is a real difference in impact that is being registered. I might have convinced a few individuals, but I didn't move the whole group to a new level of understanding."

He inquires: "How could you tell? What were the signs?"

"Little things," I say. "In Bern, on the surface, the presentation was uneventful. Some of the listeners were interested, and a few, like you, even appreciative. But I think that the bulk of the listeners were thoroughly puzzled. It probably seemed to them an apocalyptic vision. It would bring imminent dislocation and difficulty. It was too different, too new. They had heard about the Web, but few had experienced it. They were apprehensive at my exuberance. They were nervous that I might open the sluice gates of the future and drown their habitual patterns of action. They assumed that this vision was something for others, not for themselves. They couldn't imagine how their small conservative organization could possibly evolve in such a fashion. In suggesting a digital revolution, I was seen as a messenger from a technological hell. Even the Yemen story, which usually works so well, left them with more questions than answers."

He looks at me with a wry smile. He is used to getting these kinds of lectures. "You have to realize," he says, "that here in Bern, we have an image of technological obsolescence. We feel that we are way behind."

"Only by months."

"I'm not sure people here really want to catch up," he says. "The vision is too overwhelming, too much of a stretch. It's jarring rather than harmonizing. They see it as too much of a leap. In any event, don't worry—some of the audience got it."

"The problem is," I say, "there's an immense difference between one or two individuals getting it, and a whole group springing to a new level of understanding, together. This is what happened in London and what hasn't occurred here in Bern. The presentation in London resonated intensely and lifted many in the audience to a new level of understanding about the use of storytelling. In Bern, it was the same presentation as I had given in London, and yet it didn't resonate to the same extent. They just weren't ready."

"Why was that?" he asks.

"I'm not sure," I say, "Perhaps in London, the beginning situation was very different. Everyone had come to London with an interest, greater or smaller, in learning about how to share knowledge and was struggling with various aspects of it. There was a community of shared assumptions about the possibility of value in it, of a wish to learn more about implementation, a convergence of purpose. They had spent a whole day together hearing everyone agonize about the struggle and how difficult it was. They were ready to learn. Here in Bern, by contrast, the participants were there because they had been instructed to come. There was no convergent purpose. There were the mixed agendas related to the question of succession in the organization. It was a struggle for the future of the organization, the fight for its soul. In their questions, people were saying that they didn't want to see their future in terms of technology."

"That wasn't your message," he says.

"It doesn't matter. That's what they read into it. In London, what I hoped that they would get out of it and what the bulk of the listeners understood had met in one place. One felt that almost everyone spontaneously and at the same time co-created the same story in their minds. The audience response, the laughter, the questions, the conversation afterwards—the convergence occurred, and everyone felt it. As a result, the presentation was more than several hundred individuals independently having the identical subjective experience. The stories being generated during the presentation were held in place by the recognition that hundreds of others were co-creating essentially the same story in their minds. The co-created stories were not merely independent mental events. The whole was larger than the parts."

"Did it really matter how many people got it or not?" he asks.

"I think so. In London an identical story was being co-created and responded to by other listening individuals at the same time. The participants were aware of the fact of the simultaneous co-creation. For each participant, the story co-created was subjective. Yet each participant could not help being aware of the general receptiveness. Each listener was aware of the acceptance of the concepts by other thinking individuals. The resulting emergence of meaning went beyond individual thinking. Participants grasped that storytelling would be one of the ways of coping with the world. It will be seen as sensible, intelligent, necessary, a lens through which they would see the world. That was what didn't happen here in Bern."

"Are you sure about all this?" he asks.

"No, of course I'm not, but all the signs were there that we didn't get this effect here. Stories work well when a group becomes open to the flow of a larger intelligence. There's a physicist called David Bohm who speculated that thought itself is not the result of an individual in isolation, but is largely a collective phenomenon. A story creates a dialogue-like space in a free flow of meaning that passes and moves through and between people, in the sense of a stream that flows between the banks. As in dialogue, a group accesses a large pool of common meaning that cannot be fully accessed individually."[3]

"In addition, you were a visitor," he says.

"Here today and gone tomorrow. My vision isn't obviously rooted in anything Swiss. I am ephemeral, a transitory flash. I don't connect with anything local."

"Don't blame yourself," he says. "No one could have done any better."

"Perhaps not," I say, "without spending more time understanding the current issues, mingling with the people, getting in harmony with the existing situation. Then in the presentation, I would have needed

---

3 David Bohm, *On Dialogue.* London and New York: Routledge, 1996, p. 14.

a better definition of the problem as they themselves saw it, and created a story that was better adapted to the local scene."

"It's up to us to follow up," he says.

"Let me know if I can help," I say.

We follow on with the usual perfunctory things one says at these moments—about how good it has been to see each other again, and how we are going to remain in contact, although we both know we have no intention or even time to stick to the promises. We will put our parallel futures in the hands of destiny, which will bring us together again, as it has so many times over the years, without our making any special effort.

⌣

This night, I dine alone and somewhat morosely in the hotel restaurant. My presentation has misfired, but there is nothing to be done about it.

I can imagine what has been happening in Bern in multiple conversations in the white vinyl offices—or over dinner tables of *raclette* or *roesti* potatoes—ever since my presentation. People will be talking about the stories of their day, stories about the past, the present and the future, and in this way, creating the meaning that is necessary for them to operate with any degree of effectiveness. The collective communicative life of the individuals in the agency I have just visited will involve the exchange of experiences, fears, and dreams. I have no way of knowing how what I was saying today will flow into this large underground current of communication.

I do know that the outcome of today's presentation will depend on what story is told by the participants to each other and to their colleagues. The story that is told is not peripheral or an insignificant froth on the surface, but the true lifeblood of the living organization. It is the shared stories that hold the organization together: the organizational structures and management contraptions are merely the tools that operate at the stories' behest.

The message of global economic change and the story of Yemen will be thrown into this current of underground communication. The hostility to technology will be a stiff countercurrent, and my stories might well sink, never to be heard of again. Or they might become translated into a power play for the management succession in the organization. Or they might be picked up by some and used to illustrate the positive possibilities that lie ahead for the agency. The multiple currents will cause these stories to bob about and be carried along by the force of the flow and counterflow of the ongoing communication.

One thing is certain. The stories of my presentation will be transformed into a story with a different meaning from what I presented or intended. Storytelling can sometimes enable a communication to bypass the defenses of an unreceptive audience. This works by adopting precisely the methods adopted by the underground current of communication. It happened in London. But here in Bern, the stories that will spring forth at the end of the session are not likely to be the progeny that I had wanted to spawn. The resulting meaning of this new set of stories will thus be different from the explicit words that were transmitted. Where there are too many agendas in play, even a story will not necessarily be successful. If the purposes are too disparate, the springboard doesn't spring. The listeners stay earthbound with all their current assumptions.

All I could do is to throw my story into this river of communication and hope for the best. I could not control the flow. I could not even determine where the flow would carry it. As a visitor, I am a short-lived stimulus who would be soon gone. The only measure of the success of the presentation is what stories people are telling to each other. Bern has shown me the limits. A story is not a panacea.

# SEVEN

# Another Mode of Knowing

*A single map is but one of an indefinitely large number of maps that might be produced for the same situation or from the same data.*

Mark Monmonier, *How to Lie with Maps*[1]

**B**y the following morning, much of the pristine white snow that coincided with my arrival in Bern is sliding from tree limbs and steep roofs, and the city's streets are awash with slush and muck, haphazardly kicked up by passing buses and trucks to speckle the jacket of the unsuspecting traveler. I am not unhappy to be quitting the muddy gutters of Switzerland and to be flying home to Washington.

Unlike the confined and murky night-world of the eastward flight, the view from the window of my 747 on the westward leg across the Atlantic is bathed in the blinding white sunshine of a seemingly endless day. Beneath a canopy of pure unchanging blue, the clarity of that altitude lifts my spirits, as if the atmosphere has been rinsed of all misunderstanding.

As we reach our cruising altitude, the pilot introduces himself over the airplane's intercom and says that the temperature outside is an icy minus fifty-five degrees. The blonde-haired flight attendant provides me with a glass of chilled white wine with a smile. With such

[1] Mark S. Monmonier, *How to Lie with Maps*. Chicago: University of Chicago Press, 1991, p. 2.

inspiration in hand, I throw a glance at the unlimited visibility outside, stretching into the distance, almost infinite.

From such a vantage point, I think how easy it would be to construct a map of the Alps, whose silvery white peaks are at this time sliding by below me. Where ancient cartographers had struggled for centuries to capture the undulating contours of the earth's surface, I can from where I sit grasp the major relationships of entire mountain ranges in a single glance. How easy it would be to mark the path Hannibal and his caravan of elephants followed in crossing the Alps, or the one by which Caesar stormed his way into Gaul! From this wonderful position of aboveness, it is easy to believe in the perfection of the intelligible, the measurable, and the mapped, and to be skeptical of the fantastic, the vague, and the shapeless.[2]

Of course, if Sven Birkerts were sitting with me, he would be regretting the excellence of our technology that means that the physical aspect of our planet no longer conceals any secrets from us. There will no longer be any need for the medieval mapmakers and their delicate vellum sketches, replete with swirling curlicues, cherub-faced winds, multiarmed men, and miraculous imaginary animals, inscribed along the side. Less fanciful but more accurate maps are now everywhere at hand. Satellites routinely track the movements of the winds and clouds and hurricanes. Computer printouts immediately reproduce extremely minute details. In this fashion, the mysteries of all known lands have already been unraveled. No undiscovered countries lie just over the horizon. The surface of the earth has almost nothing left to reveal.

But if this simple physical mystery no longer exists, other more complex puzzles surely await the mapmaker's talents. With the physical contours of our planet so perfectly represented, what remains for mapmakers but to turn their attentions to the virtual journeys and

---

[2] Camille Paglia, *Sexual Personae: Art and Decadence from Nefertiti to Emily Dickinson*. New Haven: Yale University Press, 1990, p. 73.

excursions of the mind? There are still many virtual domains beyond all known frontiers, strange and wonderful places that speak of unlimited possibilities.

I learned from Sven Birkerts of the virtual journeys in which readers engage when they follow a story. In the same way, the listeners in my audiences traveled with me to Kamana, Zambia, and relived the experience of the health worker searching for an answer to a question on how to treat malaria. Or visited with the task team in Chile as they advised the client on the global experience of coping with teachers' unions. Or were present with the task team in Yemen advising on education information systems. On hearing these stories, listeners proceeded to create new journeys of their own that they followed in their own minds and imaginations. Is there some way I could plot the paths that they had taken?

Could we map what these listeners had learned on these virtual journeys? Could we map the worlds they had co-created in their imaginations? Could we depict what they had envisioned in their mind's eye?

Birkerts had encouraged me to concentrate on the actual journey itself as the principal thing of value. Yet surely quality could also pervade a map of the journey. Without claiming to duplicate the freshness and intensity of the actual journey, a map could at least be accurate and portable.

The internal world of storytelling had already given us hints about the nature of these virtual journeys, how ideas are created and then re-created in different minds. I had learned much about *how* stories have the effect that they have, and I could appreciate the subtle weavings of these interactions. But there is also the question of *what* is occurring when storytelling was having its effect. What knowledge is involved? We know that listeners are adding content. It isn't just the twenty-nine words that are having this reaction. What exactly is being added?

I reach beneath my seat and take from my leather briefcase the slides that I had picked up at the London conference. As I look at them, I smile. They are like the slides from any of the knowledge conferences I have attended. They have one thing in common. They are all obscure, mechanistic, and lifeless. The concept of organizational change that I have been trying to depict is of complex phenomena, as multifaceted and quick-changing and organic as the organization in which it is being implemented. The idea is growing dynamically over time, fuzzy, curved, bulging, blossoming, struggling, more like a new kind of life form than any simple linear abstraction, just as the organization itself continues its awesome capacity to morph. But the slides I am looking at convey a very different image. The organizations represented here look simple and linear and mechanistic. They are full of straight lines and sharp angles like a lifeless plastic artifact manufactured by a factory. So these charts are subliminally conveying something quite different from the pictures of living things, which are all curves and fractals and ambiguity. Since there are no straight lines in nature, the slides with their straight lines are implicitly conveying the message that the subject matter—the organizations of which they are talking—comprises unnatural artifacts, ideas that had never been alive, and could not be alive in the form in which they are shown in these slides. As maps, they are very inaccurate.

I recall other books I had consulted, such as Edward Tufte's wonderful treatises on the visual depiction of complex information, including the occasional masterpiece such as the chart showing Napoleon's march into Russia, and his subsequent retreat.[3] But even here, we are talking about a completed event that is being represented, not a living, breathing, evolving concept. Again, it is a record of a postmortem, something that is already dead. In general, the charts shown there do not hold much promise of representing the kind of living complexity that I am trying to represent.

A more plausible line of inquiry seems to lie in the mathematical representations of complexity. These maps have a distinguished

---

[3] Edward R. Tufte, *The Visual Display of Quantitative Information.* Cheshire, CT: Graphics Press, 1983, p. 41.

genealogy, starting with René Descartes, the French philosopher and mathematician of the seventeenth century. Among Descartes's many achievements was his success in unifying the traditions of geometry and algebra. Geometry was developed by the ancient Greeks and adopted by the founder of modern science, Galileo, in his systematic experiments. Its components were triangles, circles, and other geometric figures. Algebra was developed several centuries after the ancient Greeks, by Islamic philosophers in Persia, who had learned it from Indian mathematicians. Algebra enabled the description of different variables in symbolic form and the solution of straightforward equations.

Descartes was the first to map the journey of a point in motion and so unify the approaches of geometry and algebra. His system involved assigning the coordinates of a point on horizontal and vertical axes. This enabled the plotting of relationships in two-dimensional space, including both linear relationships (where inputs were proportional to outputs) and nonlinear relationships (where inputs were not proportional to outputs, because one or several of the variables were squared or raised to higher powers).

In due course, Newton and Leibniz developed differential calculus, and Newton used it in his equations of motion to describe the movement of solid bodies at variable speeds, accelerating or slowing down. The equations of motion were used to describe the movements of the solar system, planets, moons, and comets, as well as the flow of tides and other phenomena related to gravity, and it was progressively applied to other spheres.

Newton's equations of motion were very general and applicable to both linear and nonlinear phenomena. But since the nonlinear equations were too difficult at that time to be solved, there was a tendency to replace them with linear approximations. Thus, instead of describing the phenomena in their full complexity, the equations of classical science dealt with small oscillations, shallow waves, small changes in temperature, and so on. This habit became so strong that many equations were linearized while they were being set up, so that the science textbooks did not even include the full nonlinear versions. Consequently, most scientists and engineers came to think of complex natural phenomena as being more or less accurately described by linear equations. Just as the world was viewed as clockwork for the eighteenth century, so the picture of the world for the nineteenth and most of the twentieth century was insistently linear.[4]

To the extent that nonlinear phenomena were plotted, they were marked on Descartes's charts with his system of coordinates. This was adequate to depict the relationship of two variables. But the problem was that most complex systems had many variables. Such systems were too difficult to depict or visualize. As a result, the scientific world gradually became a huge and unrealistic oversimplification of the subject being studied, so that people began to think of things as being generally linear or with a strictly limited numbers of variables. In other words, there was a big gap between the mental maps in use and reality.

The decisive change in science over the last several decades of the twentieth century has been to recognize that nature is pervasively nonlinear, with multiple variables interacting on each other. Nonlinear multivariate phenomena dominate even the inanimate world, and they are obviously an essential aspect of living systems.

More recently, scientists have built on the work the French mathematician Poincaré. Utilizing newly created computing power, they have worked out methodologies for representing such relationships at least mathematically. In this approach, each variable is represented by a coordinate in a different dimension in phase space. If there are sixteen variables, we have—mathematically represented—a sixteen-dimensional space. A single point in that space will describe the state of the entire system completely, because this single point has sixteen

---

4 Ian Stewart. *Does God Play Dice: The Mathematics of Chaos.* Oxford, UK; New York: B. Blackwell, 1989, p. 83.

coordinates, and each corresponds to one of the system's sixteen variables or dimensions.

This might be satisfactory for mathematical description, but the problem for communication is that we cannot visualize a phase space with sixteen dimensions. We can instantly grasp two dimensions, as shown by Descartes. Three variables can be understood reasonably easily, through drawings sketched with perspective. Even four dimensions of coordinates are manageable using sequential sketches of variables in three-dimensional space. But as we move beyond that, we quickly find ourselves in trouble. This is why it is called abstract mathematical space. Mathematicians might not have any problems in visualizing such abstractions. But the average person certainly does. So in theory the chart can describe mathematically complex phenomena, but in practice it cannot communicate the complexity of the phenomena being described. As a mathematical tool, it is brilliant. As a communications tool for the non-mathematician, it is a catastrophe.

But if we can agree to relax the communication constraint on our problem, we can at least begin to see what the map of the story's content might correspond to.

Although sixteen-dimensional space is unimaginable, the paths of natural phenomena tend to be patterned, not random, and rotating around attractors. One striking fact about attractors is that they tend to be of very low dimensionality, even in a high-dimensional phase space. For example, a system might have sixteen variables, but its motion may be restricted to an attractor of three dimensions, a folded surface in that sixteen-dimensional space.[5]

Even though the system can generally be described in multiple dimensions, one cannot predict which particular point it will pass through at a specific time. As a result, we end up making predictions

5 Fritjof Capra, *The Web of Life: A New Scientific Understanding of Living Systems*. New York: Anchor Books, 1996, pp. 125–132.

not about precise values, but rather about qualitative features of the system's behavior. This can be represented in simple two-dimensional drawings known as phase portraits.[6]

This line of reasoning provides a key to another puzzle. If non-linear phenomena dominate the world of both living and nonliving things, and if we have only recently developed the mathematical sophistication to deal with such phenomena, and if even these techniques are well nigh useless for the purposes of communication, how on earth has the human race coped with complex nonlinear phenomena all these millennia? How do we understand what is going on? How do we communicate about it?

A major part of the answer is narrative.[7] One reason why we live in a soup of narratives, why narratives permeate our lives and understanding, is that resorting to narratives is the way in which we have learned to cope with our world of enormously complex phenomena. Even while scientists and schoolteachers have been telling us to abandon these unscientific approaches, and adopt linear abstract thinking, the human race has used its common sense and stubbornly—to some extent surreptitiously—stuck with narratives as the most

---

[6] Capra, p. 133.

[7] A further part of the answer lies in the vagueness or fuzziness of natural language. "The science of the nineteenth century was like its philosophy, its morals and its civilization in general, distinguished by a certain hardness, primness and precise limitation and demarcation of ideas. *Vagueness,* indefinite and blurred outlines, anything savoring of mysticism, was abhorrent to that great age of limited exactitude. The rigid categories of physics were applied to the indefinite and hazy phenomena of life and mind. Concepts were in logic as well as science narrowed down to their most luminous points, and the rest of the contents treated as non-existent.... The world is thus in [bivalent] abstraction constituted of entities that are discontinuous, with nothing between them to bridge the impassable gulfs, little or great, that separate them from each other. The world becomes to us a mere collection of *disjecta membra,* drained of all union or mutual relations, dead, barren, inactive, unintelligible. And in order once more to bring relations into this scrap heap of disconnected entities, the mind has to conjure up spirits, influences, forces and what not from the vast deep of its own imagination." Jan Christiaan Smuts, *Holism and Evolution* (New York, The Macmillan Company, 1926) cited in Bart Kosko, *Fuzzy Thinking: The New Science of Fuzzy Logic.* New York: Hyperion, 1993, p. 138.

usable tool to cope with complexity. We have used the narrative language of stories as the most appropriate instrument to communicate the nature and shape and behavior of complex adaptive phenomena. Stories capture the essence of living things, which are quintessentially complex phenomena, with multiple variables, unpredictable phase changes, and all of the characteristics that the mathematics of complexity has only recently begun to describe. The fact that narratives are not mathematically precise, and in fact are full of fuzzy qualitative relationships, seems to be a key to their success in enabling us to cope with complexity. The story form has been used to record and communicate the activities of complex inanimate phenomena—the weather, disease, war, the stock market, commodity prices—as a shorthand way of making things intelligible that are not comprehensible by any other means.

Of course, narrative is only an analogy and hence partially inaccurate, but no more of an analogy than a linear equation or one of Descartes's charts. For most purposes, as a description of complex adaptive systems, narratives are considerably more accurate than Descartes's charts.

In fact, some distortion is inevitable in the very act of description or mapmaking.

> *Not only is it easy to lie with maps. It is essential. To portray meaningful relationships for a complex, three-dimensional world on a flat sheet of paper or a video screen, a map must distort reality. As a scale model, the map must use symbols that almost always are proportionally much bigger or thicker than the features they represent. To avoid hiding critical information in a fog of detail, the map must offer a selective, incomplete view of reality. There's no escape from the cartographic paradox: to present a useful and truthful picture, an accurate map must tell white lies.*[8]

---

[8] Monmonier, p. 1.

Misdescription is built into the very nature of mapmaking. No single map can ever be completely accurate. In making the selection, the map is necessarily a misrepresentation.

Any single map is but one of an indefinitely large number of maps that might be produced for the same situation or from the same data.[9] Any situation might be the subject of different maps, all of which are inaccurate in different ways. Understanding the specific inaccuracies of a map is a key to understanding its value as a map. It's a matter of choosing—and being willing to live with—the inaccuracies for the purposes you had in mind.

⌐⌐

Armed with these insights, and some more white wine from the fair-haired flight attendant, I now have a clearer understanding of what has been going on. Thus, in trying to create a visual map that conveys the immense complexity of an evolving concept such as knowledge management, I have, unwittingly, been aping the behavior of the scientists of the nineteenth and the first part of the twentieth centuries, who insisted on depicting complex nonlinear phenomena with simple linear pictures, or isolating one or two variables from a phenomenon that had ten or twenty variables.[10] My two dimensional charts are at best partial truths of much more complex phenomena. They can reflect a few dimensions of a multidimensioned reality. As I add more dimensions to capture more of the reality, I find, as the scientists found, that the chart collapses into incomprehensibility at about the fourth dimension.

So in response to the question as to whether the failure of my charts to communicate is due to my map-drawing capacity or to the

---

9 Monmonier, p. 2.

10 Knowledge management might be seen as comprising multiple dimensions, including knowledge strategy, communities of practice, help desks, knowledge bases, knowledge capture, knowledge storage, knowledge dissemination, knowledge taxonomies, quality assurance, authentication procedures, budget, incentives, and knowledge measures.

whole idea of drawing maps to describe complex multidimensional problems, I am able to conclude that it is the latter.

The underlying problem is that the nature of what I am trying to describe—the world of organizations—is complex, messy, fuzzy, irregular, asymmetrical, random, in continuous disequilibrium. These phenomena cannot be depicted simply in two-dimensional charts.

The same reasoning provides a clue as to why organizations can seem both orderly and chaotic. Organizations resemble other complex adaptive systems. In some respects, they are chaotic, turbulent, but in other respects, they have predictable, structured patterns, analogous to the swirling whirlpool of water that we see when we watch the bathwater disappear down the plughole. The general structure of the form is highly predictable, but the specific phenomena involved as reflected in the equations of the forces at play are immensely complicated and apparently haphazard.

I can also see why management textbooks don't talk about organizations as complex, messy, fuzzy, irregular, asymmetrical, random, in continuous disequilibrium—because in our intellectual tradition, these are all seen as bad things. Our whole culture tells us that they are wrong. Since the Greeks, we have been led to believe that the world is like Euclidean geometry, if only we could understand it right—with straight lines and sharp angles, and simple linear phenomena—along with the subtle implication that it *ought* to be like that. The good things in life are clear, simple, clean, orderly, neat. If it isn't exactly so, then it should be made to look that way, at least in pictures.

Yet we intuitively know that the world is not this way. Our world is full of complex adaptive systems. They are everywhere we look—people, organizations, economies, animals, plants, weather—anything that is worth a damn is a complex adaptive system. And we intuitively use stories to communicate the complexity that is all around us. This is why stories are ubiquitous. It is only when we try to get serious that our minds freeze over, our schoolteacher-induced mindsets take over, and we start talking in linear terms about complex phenomena and drawing two-dimensional maps of our thoughts. At best, these are partial truths. Often they are sheer nonsense.

An understanding of the nature of maps can help to overcome our sense of surprise and disbelief when we first learn that narratives turn out to be more apt than analysis for the communication of very complex ideas. The reason is simple. Narratives are a better fit not only with the way our brains are made, but also with the underlying reality of the subject matter being discussed.

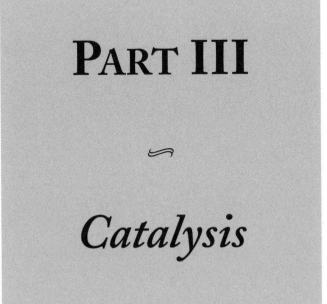

# PART III

## Catalysis

# EIGHT

# Crafting the Springboard Story

*A story that makes sense is one that stirs the senses from their slumber, one that opens the eyes and ears to their real surroundings, running the tongue in the actual tastes in the air and sending chills of recognition along the surface of the skin. To make sense is to release the body from the constraints imposed by outworn ways of speaking, and hence to renew and rejuvenate one's felt awareness of the world. It is to make the senses wake up to where they are.*

David Abrams, *The Spell of the Sensuous*[1]

*Ideas are not the sum and substance of thought; rather, thought is as much about the motion across the water as it is about the stepping stones that allow it.*

Sven Birkerts, *The Gutenberg Elegies*[2]

The spring of 1998. It has been a difficult winter. If I look back on the months that follow my return from London and Bern, the thing that sticks in memory is how busy we are—giddy, dizzying non-stop activity. Dashing hither and thither, organizing the knowledge management board, explaining yet again the case for change, preparing budget instructions, making up tables and matrices, doing individual one-

---

[1] David Abram, *The Spell of the Sensuous: Perception and Language in a More-than-Human World.* New York: Pantheon Books, 1997, p. 265.

[2] Sven Birkerts, *The Gutenberg Elegies: The Fate of Reading in an Electronic Age.* Boston: Faber and Faber, 1994, p. 11.

on-ones, getting together with vice presidents, having working lunch-
es with budget officers, convening the leaders of communities of practice, running focus groups, organizing retreats, or talking to potential
partners.

If I ask myself what all this activity is for, I cannot always answer
with accuracy. The Yemen presentation of December 1997 has created
the positive frame for making progress: what remains is to complete
the details within the frame. Despite the fresh consensus on knowledge sharing, getting specific decisions for implementation is something else. The issues come at us in clusters.

Number one is the budget for knowledge management which has
been diverted from its intended purpose. For knowledge sharing to be
successful, the money has to be recovered. It is the lifeblood of the
communities of practice that we are trying to nurture into some kind
of viability. The change involves moving money from one unit's budget
to another's. The action is rational—but each of the units contains
people, and people have feelings: in moving money around, the emotional quotient is high. For an organization such as ours that largely
governs itself by means of the budget, having the money is an indis-
pensable emblem of institutional acceptance. The fact of a transfer
from one unit to another is perceived as a blow to those who will no
longer have control over it. It is as if a set of banners and flags are being
hauled down in one castle and raised aloft somewhere else. Even
people who fundamentally agree with each other speak in tones that
are less than objective. The discussion is not so much about money as
about what the money has come to represent.

The organizational choreography involved in getting a complex
set of activities to take place under one budget rubric rather than
another is intricate, with a sequence of movement, transition, and
repose just as elaborate as the orchestration of a dance.

The Yemen story has provided the music, but the exact steps have
to be written and executed by a large number of players, proceeding
unit by unit, with instructions that are clear enough until everyone
is—more or less—operating off the same score, with the same tune,

and same rhythm. In the end, the deed is done. Figures representing sums of money are officially inscribed in one column rather than another, and everyone understands what that means. But once it is done, egos need to be bandaged. Wounded feelings have to be soothed. Such hurts don't heal immediately and may cut a furrow in memory for months, perhaps years, to come.

We operate opportunistically. The hectic breathless nature of the situation means accepting even seemingly unpromising opportunities to win more supporters to the cause. We never know when the next chance for takeoff will come. And if some things lead nowhere, others have serendipitous benefits that could not have been anticipated.

To exploit the opportunities, we need more stories. Up to this point, our search for stories has been haphazard. We wander around talking to people we happen to meet. These meetings create leads and eventually a story is cobbled together. Now we ask ourselves: what will happen if we become more systematic?

So we recruit two staff specifically to help us develop more stories.

A couple of days after their starting to work, I ask them how things are going. They say: not well. I ask them why not. They explain that they can't just go into a unit and ask for stories and expect to be accepted, with people suddenly opening up. Things don't work that way. They have to make themselves known, find out what is going on, and get familiar with the context. In effect, they are finding what every anthropologist has found before them: they are having difficulty in getting acceptance and entrée.

So we provide them with an escort, to get the door open—someone to help set up the interview, participate, and cement the social connections. This enables them to use us as a calling card.

But even so, they are puzzled. "What exactly do I want? What kind of stories?"

I reply that until I see the stories, I don't really know. I can give some examples more easily than principles.

"Do I mean stories exactly like Chile or Yemen?"

"No, not exactly, just analogous. Stories that will show how knowledge sharing is working, on the front lines, in the trenches. Stories that are embedded in their context."

The staff are not really satisfied with my explanation, but at this stage I cannot do any better, and they set out on their task.

〜

A few weeks pass, and I chat with them to see whether they have come up with any good stories. They say: "Not yet." I remind them that time is flying by. We are almost at the midpoint of their brief assignment with us.

They insist that they are not ready.

I inquire whether I can get an advance draft of what they are working on, but still they say: not even that.

I surmise that they have something done but are reluctant to share it with me, worried in case it isn't up to snuff. So I use the excuse of an imminent trip to issue a friendly ultimatum and ask them to try their respective hands at an initial draft of a story on something or someone that they have discovered to date, and to do this before the weekend, and to give it to me, ready or not. In this way I can give them feedback and we will be able to get into an interactive mode. Even if their work is rough I tell them that I want to see it, come what may. In the process, I am thinking that I will discover what I myself really want, and we will all learn in the process how to proceed.

Friday arrives, and they submit their draft. As I suspect, it is not at all what I want. In fact, they have not provided me with stories, but rather third-person accounts of some insights that they have come up with as a result of their stay to date. There are references to incidents, but they are not in a form that would enable anyone else to understand the implications. There is not enough plot to see how the content is relevant. The references lack specifics. They lack names. They lack dates. Above all, they lack pizzazz. The staff are describing a bureaucratic environment. I want something different. I want an account that will enable people to relive the story of sharing knowledge. I suggest that maybe they should turn themselves into journalists and start looking for something new and writing it up as a newspaper story.

Then the staff confess that they are still not sure precisely what I want or what they are meant to be looking for. Or how to go about finding stories like Chile or Yemen.

I can see that I will have to be clearer as to what I mean.

*Let's take an example that we've used recently, as it happens, from the Central African Republic.*

*In 1997, a task manager in the Central African Republic was confronted with a problem. He had been asked to advise the Government on an aspect of privatization of a local phone company. The question was: how to deal with a minority shareholder who retains a right of first refusal? As it happened, the task manager didn't know what had been done on similar issues in other countries. In the past, what would have occurred is that the task manager would promise to get back to the Government once he returned to Washington and could research the issue.*

*Now, with knowledge management, he was able to contact the community of practice by email and ask for urgent help. In Washington, D.C., the leader of the community of practice was able to provide him by email with a similar Kenyan experience in the telecommunications industry. This happened the same day. The coordinator also copied his answer to the rest of the community of practice and asked them to share directly their own experiences with the task manager. As a result, in Washington, D.C., on the same day, an additional insight was sent to the task manager in the Central African Republic. It was the experience of pre-emptive rights from unexpected source in a different sector—the oil industry in Morocco. The elapsed time was 11 hours.*

*As a result, the next morning at ten o'clock the task manager in the Central African Republic was able, on the basis of experience that he had learned about in Morocco and Kenya, to advise our client on this aspect of privatizing the local phone company. The overall elapsed time was less than 24 hours to help solve a complicated problem in which the actors were scattered over the globe and the relevant know-how was located in unexpected places.*

*Now that the experience has been identified as valuable, it can be captured and stored in the electronic knowledge base for use by others— inside or outside the organization—who are confronted with a similar issue.*

I explain to the staff that stories like this have a certain shape and form. There are three essential keys. Of these, the third most important element is connectedness.

CONNECTEDNESS: THE STORY, HOWEVER CONDENSED, HAS TO LINK THE AUDIENCE WITH A POSITIVE CONTROLLING IDEA AND A PROTAGONIST WITH WHOM THE AUDIENCE EMPATHIZES.

The central figure in the story from the Central African Republic is not the person who told us what happened—the coordinator of the community of practice, whose advice was being sought. It is difficult to empathize with an apparently desk-bound knowledge provider. The story is told instead from the point of view of the task manager who is stranded—without the right expertise when he needs it—in one of the world's most out-of-the-way places—the city of Bangui in central Africa.

For audiences in our organization, it is the ability and willingness to empathize with the protagonist who is desperately in need of some know-how in an out-of-the-way place that helps give the story its springboard effect. It is the predicament of the protagonist that begins to create the imaginative sympathy that transports the listener—virtually—to this distant land. The trick is to get the listeners to put themselves mentally in the shoes of the protagonist.

For the story to have broad impact, it is important that the protagonist be someone who plays a typical role in the business of our particular organization. If we were a sales organization, the ideal protagonist would be a salesman. If we were a manufacturing organization, the ideal protagonist would be in manufacturing. In the stories that have worked in our organization, the protagonist is almost always someone in operations—a leader of a multidisciplinary task team in some out-of-the-way place, since this is how the work of our organization gets done, the terrain where the idea of knowledge sharing will either live or die.

It is through empathy for the protagonist in difficulty that the audience's emotions become engaged, and so get to a deeper level of meaning. For this to happen, the audience has to feel something for the story's protagonist. Hence, the more remote and apparently difficult the predicament, the more likely this connectedness is to occur. If the protagonist in the Central African Republic had been, for instance, at headquarters in Washington when he asked for advice, the story might not have the same impact.

Note also that the Central African Republic story is told from the perspective of a single protagonist. The drafts prepared by the staff feature a number of different participants without adopting the perspective of anyone in particular. Stories with multiple protagonists are more difficult to craft so as to win the listeners' sympathy. In this respect, the principles of constructing narratives diverge from the principles of assembling evidence. In generating evidence, the more instances and witnesses one can produce of a phenomenon, the stronger the evidence is usually considered to be. Narratives operate in the opposite manner. They engage the listeners' imagination and emotions through an understanding of an individual's specific predicament.

The dynamic of the interaction of a story with the listener depends on an initial problem that draws the audience into the story. Once the audience understands enough about the protagonist and the initial quandary, they tend to be "hooked" by the conflict. Then the storyteller can proceed with the events that lead to the resolution.

In the Central African Republic story, the audience in our organization understands the plight of a task manager not having an answer in a country like the Central African Republic, with apparently no one on hand to help. The audience has enough understanding of the predicament to be connected to the story.

By contrast, the same story told in a different organization might fail to connect, as in Bern. For outsiders without the background, the response could be very different. It can be a shrug and a "So what?"

They may not understand enough of the background for the incident to grab them. They don't see the meaning. There is not enough connectedness with the audience.

*STRANGENESS: THE SPRINGBOARD STORY MUST VIOLATE THE LISTENER'S EXPECTATIONS IN SOME WAY.*

As I look at the first work of the staff, I can see that they have another problem. They are too mundane, too ordinary—they are not striking enough. They are boring. The situation has to be intelligible, through a familiar predicament, but it also has to be unusual.

The second most important element of the springboard story is that it has to involve a certain element of surprise or incongruity. It has to violate the listeners' perceptual frameworks in some way. The violation interrupts the thought process of the listeners either because there is a new event that is not expected, or because an expected event that does not happen.[3]

In the Central African Republic, the normal outcome in the past would have been for the task team leader to say to the client posing an unexpected request: we'll get back to you. What actually happened was something different. The task team leader found the answer within 24 hours—a welcome but unexpected turn of events. Narratives operate on such irregularities, by identifying the unexpected and building meaning out of that. It is these irregularities by which from childhood we learn about the peculiarities of the world. By contrast, abstractions take advantage of regularities. They form the background against which the irregularities of narratives are registered.[4]

---

[3] G. Mandler, *Mind and Body: Psychology of Emotion and Stress.* New York: W.W. Norton, 1984; W.H. Starbuck, and F.J. Milliken, "Executives' perceptual filters: What they notice and how they make sense," in D.C. Hambrick, *The Executive Effect: Concepts and Methods for Studying Top Managers.* Greenwich, CT: JAI Press, 1988, pp. 35–65.

[4] Jerome Bruner, Culture and Human Development: A New Look, in *Human Development,* (1990), Vol. 33, pp. 344–355.

If the story is boring, or a cliché for the audience, with nothing unexpected occurring, they are unlikely to listen or learn. There has to be the shock of the unforeseen—such as divergent opinion, unpredictable data, sudden emotion, new characters, or unexpected relationships. An interesting story is potentially a threat to one's model of reality or frame, which means that interesting stories are cues that can evoke a mixture of fear and curiosity. They are a pretext to update our frame of understanding, even though the very novelty of their content might make it difficult to do so.[5]

In the case of the Central African Republic story, the unexpectedness lies in the ability to get expertise within 24 hours while still in Bangui.

The question of strangeness is specific to the particular audience. What is new to one is old hat to another. Only testing can determine whether something is fresh and unconventional in that setting, and enable one to judge what reception it will get in the organization or community in which the story is being told.

At the same time, the story should not be too strange. One doesn't want the audience starting to debate the details of the story. Hence, it needs to be clear enough for them to understand the process, but not so clear that they get involved in the details. One is aiming for a Rorschach inkblot phenomenon where the image is indeterminate and the input comes from the listener, so that the second story, the implicit story, gets created. Thus, in our organization, the Central African Republic story is familiar enough that the story works. In Bern, a similar story about Yemen didn't work with that audience, because the world was too strange, too different, too removed.

In the Central African Republic story, I talk about the rights of a minority shareholder, without going into the details of exactly what

---

5 Karl Weick, *Sensemaking in Organizations*. Thousand Oaks: Sage Publications, 1995, pp. 127–128; Robert Grudin, *On Dialogue: An Essay in Free Thought*. Boston: Houghton Mifflin, 1996, p. 12.

shareholding or what the problems posed by the attitude of the particular shareholder involved. The latter would risk generating a debate about minority shareholders and their problems, which is not what I want. I am trying to focus on the general principle of knowledge sharing, not the specifics of this particular instance.

The Central African Republic story works well for me, since most people know relatively little about rights of minority shareholders. This story serves better than a topic on which people have a strong personal opinion.

Making the story strange but not too strange entails a story that is close to home, but not too close. The analogy must be tight—but not too tight.

*COMPREHENSIBILITY: THE STORY HAS TO EMBODY THE IDEA SO AS TO SPRING THE LISTENER TO A NEW LEVEL OF UNDERSTANDING.*

The springboard story not only has to be strange, but it also has to be eerily familiar. If the story is too exotic, it will fail to achieve the spring to get the listeners to a new level of understanding of their own situations. For the story to achieve this effect, it has to epitomize or embody the change idea, almost like a premonition of what the future will be like. For the story to be effective with a large portion of the audience, it has to be an easy mental leap from the facts of the springboard story to a new life story of the organization that the members of the audience are potentially carrying around in their heads.

The main point of the springboard story is thus not to communicate the information contained in the springboard story itself. I do not tell the story of the Central African Republic because I want to inform people about the facts of telecommunications in that country. These facts are essentially irrelevant to my purpose, except as a pretext for getting the audience to see not only that knowledge sharing across organizational boundaries is a real possibility, but also that it could be tremendously valuable for the organization in which they work.

There are, in effect, two stories that I as the storyteller am trying to generate in the listener. One is the explicit story that the listener hears coming from the lips of the storyteller—what transpires in the Central African Republic. The other—and by far the more important—is a story that the listeners themselves will invent: a new story of how something similar to what occurred in Central African Republic could occur in the listeners' lives and work environments—a story that responds to the specific features of their specific contexts, thier problems, their hopes, and their aspirations, in terms that the listeners feel comfortable with. This second story is a creation of the listeners and cannot even be accurately imagined by the storyteller, who has no access to the necessary inputs that are in the respective heads of the listeners. And the inputs will be different for every listener. Each listener will come to the change situation with a slightly different take on the organization, a slightly different set of problems, a slightly different set of hopes and dreams for the future. If the springboard does its work properly, then the elicited story that the listeners invent will be very similar to the idea that the storyteller would like to elicit, and there will be substantial overlap between the slightly different stories that the listeners invent. The listeners will believe in the story because they have created it. Even better, because it is *their* idea, the listeners are likely to head off and persuade others that it is a great idea and start to enact the story in their own environment. The power of the springboard story therefore comes not from the story itself, but from the reaction that it elicits in the listener. The inputs of the listeners make the difference between a springboard story and a mere transmittal of information.

∽

I can see that the staff are daunted by the challenge.

"How do we go about it?" they ask.

"It's up to you. The stories have to come from an understanding gathered from living within the idea, as lived by you as participants, not merely as spectators. Finding a story means living it, breathing it, feeling it, hearing the wind rustle through it. Finally, when you are done, and you feel that you have a promising story, you have to look at it again with a fresh unprejudiced and unacademic eye. Do you see feeling in the story? The big picture matters more than the details. Is the story told with bold strokes? Is the story in accord with the big picture? Does the story have echoes of the change idea rippling through it? Is there any hint of the human spirit glimmering somewhere in the story? Does the story integrate all the disparate fragments and scintillas into a single picture of how things fit together? Does the story capture these fleeting instants to bring them into the province of the living?"[6]

I can see from the looks on their faces that they are still skeptical. They want recipes. I try to explain.

"Look at the successful stories. These are stories about people embracing and creating their future, not about following recipes. They are about abandoning recipes and returning to a world of intuition and creativity. What the stories say is: let go of structure and instructions and mechanistic guidelines and recipes and embrace your intuition and go ahead and create the future. Use the past examples, yes, but you yourself must build the new stories. Recipes risk being mechanistic. In other words, the soul of the story is more important than the specific contextual rendering.

"In your journey of creation, it can help you to know what others have done. Know how other storytellers composed their stories and perfected their methods, and find shortcuts that you might otherwise have missed. Stones to step on, and stones to avoid. But there is no purpose to be served by following any predigested recipes. These recipes may have been right for others. They made their way. But in the end, you have to make your own."[7]

---

[6] Robert Henri, *The Art Spirit.* Philadelphia and London: J. B. Lippincott Company, 1923. Reprint, New York: Harper & Row, 1984, p. 248.

[7] Henri, p. 16.

So I send the staff back to the front lines, to mingle with the people.

⤚

Shortly after this conversation, we invite all our staff, including spouses and children, to the office picnic at a country club in suburban Maryland. We step on the lawn and feel the welcome of grass beneath our feet. We sit beneath the shade of oaks and pines and for once during a weekday feel a fresh breeze on our faces. It is a fine Washington summer day, not too hot, and the kind of day when one expects little spits of rain.

One young woman, with a newly born child, has brought a guitar and sings to us charmingly. Her husband, a professional storyteller in our group, puts on a performance that helps show us the way.[8]

> *There's a prayer that I often use when I perform in different types of settings. It's a prayer that I start my performances with. It gives insight into the traditional aspect of storytelling. The prayer goes something like this. We ask for the presence of the ancestors, those who have passed away, who are not trapped by society, or this world, who know the gift of what it is to be alive. We ask for the presence of the unborn children, who are not here yet, those whose world we are creating, come and be with us and help us to prepare a world worthy of your arrival. And we ask for the presence of all of those whom we share this world with, the clouds, the trees, the mountains, the stranger on the other side of the world, the street beneath my feet, all aspects of this world, come and hold hands with me, that we may walk, leaning on each other, teaching and being taught by each other.*

---

[8] The professional storyteller is Seth Weaver Kahan. Seth tells me that he first heard the "Prayer of the Three Times" in a ceremony called the Council of All Beings in the Washington, D.C., area some years ago. A source of the prayer is Joanna Macy, *World as Lover, World as Self* (Berkeley, CA: Parallax Press, 1991), Part 4. Seth has continued to evolve the prayer to meet a variety of needs. The version of the prayer shown here is the version as performed in mid-1998.

*That prayer is called the prayer of the three times. The prayer of the ancestors, the unborn children and those whom we share the world with, lifts people up out of their daily lives and puts them in a higher context; a prayer like this, or an invocation, or a statement of purpose, is often used at the beginning of an indigenous storytelling session. What it does is scoop people up, out of the difficulties that they are facing that day, the trouble with the teenage son, or that they can't get the field to grow the crops the way they want them, and it puts them into the context of the ancestors' humanity, the human chain. What is it that I am receiving down through time? What is it that I am passing along? And then people participate in the storytelling with that set of lenses on.*

The storyteller goes on to tell the story of the old man and the bird, a story that he has told in many different settings both to entertain children and to show the meaning of knowledge management. It's a story that he first heard when he was a Boy Scout in Texas:

*There was this old man who lived in a village and he was what you would call eccentric. Most people might call him crazy, but the people in this village called him eccentric. He was really quite wise, along with his looniness, even though he could be seen wearing shorts in the wintertime, or a big fur coat in the summertime. He gave people advice about how to start a business, or raise their crops or their children in such a way that he was never wrong, and so everybody tolerated his wackiness, and went to him for advice.*

*Now there were two little boys in the village who decided to play a trick on him. Little boys have that kind of fiery energy in them, and what they decided to do was capture a small bird, and then in the town square in front of everyone, they were going to confront the old man. One of the boys was going to hold the bird behind his back, and he was going to ask the old man what he had. And if the old man could guess, then he would ask him whether it was alive or dead. If the old man said it was dead, he would let it fly away in front of everyone and make a fool of him right there on the spot. Or if he said it was alive, he would crush the bird and drop it at his feet, making a fool of him either way. That was the plan.*

*So one day when the old man was at the town square and everyone was gathered around, the little boys set about hunting. Poor baby sparrow! They captured the bird and they went up to him. When everyone was in earshot, the biggest boy held the bird and the littlest boy said, "What's my friend got behind his back?"*

*The old man looked at him a long time. That was how he had become so wise. He looked until he saw a little sparrow's feather drifting down behind the boy's legs. "Well, it's a sparrow, isn't it? A baby sparrow."*

*Everyone's eyes grew wide. But the little boy piped up just as fast, "Well, is it alive? Or is it dead?"*

*The old man looked at that boy, because he knew what he was really asking. And then he looked at the boy who was holding the bird. He looked at him until that boy looked back at him. "Well," he said, "The answer to that is in your hands."*

The children are entranced. We, the adults, even more so. Is knowledge management alive? Or is it dead? The answer is in our hands.

In this way, my friend shows us that the future of storytelling is also in our hands.

By the end of July, the effort to gather stories has been successful. We have generated a collection of some twenty-five excellent stories. We put them in a booklet and publish them in newsletters.

# NINE

# Performing the Springboard Story

PHAEDRUS: *Well, what do you think of the speech, Socrates? Isn't it a wonderful piece of work, especially the diction?*

SOCRATES: *More than wonderful, my friend, divine; it quite took my breath away. It is you who are responsible for this effect on me, Phaedrus. I concentrated on you and saw how what you were reading put you in a glow; so, believing that you know more about these things than I do, I followed your example and joined in the ecstasy, you inspired man.*

Plato, *Phaedrus,*[1]

*It is the sophist, the rhetorician, the venial orator who commit their craft to writing. The true poet is an oral rhapsode. The true thinker, the authentic pedagogue above all, relies on face-to-face speech, on the uniquely focused dynamics of direct address, as these knit question to answer and living voice to living reception.*

George Steiner, *Martin Heidegger*[2]

The idea of collecting stories during the summer of 1998 has turned out better than expected. We now have a splendid collection that our staff have furnished to us. We are publishing them one by one in newsletters. We are using them in presentations. And we make them

---

[1] Plato, *Phaedrus,* Translated by Walter Hamilton. London: Penguin Books, 1973, p. 31.

[2] George Steiner, *Martin Heidegger.* Chicago: University of Chicago Press, 1989, p. xiv.

available to those who say they need stories. Moreover, once we see the whole collection, we realize that the individual stories are interesting as stones in a mosaic, showing the varied patterns of knowledge sharing. And so the idea occurs to us to issue the whole collection in booklet form.

Then the arguments start.

When we begin circulating the collection of stories, one manager objects that his unit is not adequately represented in the collection. The stories that we have chosen from their area are not typical of what they are doing. There is too much emphasis on this, and not enough on that. I reply that these stories were never intended to be comprehensive or scientifically representative: they are intended to be illustrations, to convey examples of knowledge sharing. It is obvious that my reply is only partially successful in mollifying him.

Then I show the collection of stories to another group of staff who are actively looking for examples of knowledge management. Surely, I think, this group will find them useful. But no, they also protest at once. They want to know why the stories have such an excessive emphasis on help desks. I explain that the authors mainly worked through the staff of the help desks in gathering the material, and so naturally they came across a lot of successes through that medium. Again, it seems that my reply does not entirely satisfy them.

When a story is incorporated in a newsletter, we find that the readers consider it no more than interesting: the story doesn't appear to change basic perceptions. It evokes curiosity, but no detectable enthusiasm.

More important, when we distribute the collected stories in a booklet to various groups, we do not discern any impact at all. We find that people either do not read the booklet or read it and say: "So what?" The brochure of collected stories doesn't energize anyone. It lights no fires of excitement.

Video is no different from print in its ineffectiveness. We engage professional help to translate our presentation on to videotape, but the impact is no greater than that of the booklet.

These events give me pause. Until now, I have been struck by the importance and force of stories. Ergo, I have been thinking that if one story has an impact, a lot of stories should have even greater reverberations. Yet, we find to our disappointment that without the oral telling of the stories, the written collections of stories and case studies do not have the capacity to generate transformation.

Then it dawns on me. The stories in printed form have a very different reality from the stories in performance as they had been told. The stories in printed form can be studied as we study a bus timetable, a series of times of arrivals and departures, a kind of logarithmic table that we can look up. As such, the stories may be scarcely more alive than the abstract reasoning for which we have set them aside. To create the springboard impact, people have to live within the stories. In following a story, our understanding is not of some material object that we observe, some artifact that we set apart in our mind. In performance, the object and subject can become one; storyteller's mind, story, and listener, one inseparable unity.

The force of the story is not in the story in itself, but in its telling. When we listen to a story, the imagining that occurs is observed, as it were, from the inside. When we tell stories, we express understanding, and elicit understanding as a participant. A focus on the story alone, to the exclusion of the interaction between the storyteller and the listener, misses the point of storytelling. It is the interaction of the storyteller with the listeners and the communal meaning that emerges from the interaction.

And so our attention shifts to performance. We start thinking about how to maximize the impact of the storytelling performance. One such occasion of multiple storytelling was created serendipitously.

*INFORMAL STORYTELLING: KNOWLEDGE FAIRS CAN CREATE MULTIPLE OPPORTUNITIES FOR INFORMAL STORYTELLING.*

When I first hear early in 1998 of the idea to launch a knowledge fair, I think, as one usually does when one hears of a good new idea for the very first time: "What a wrong-headed thought!" I ask myself: "How could our extraordinarily formal and serious organization go for something so shallow and insubstantial as a fair?"

The idea is countercultural in the extreme and obviously still-born. In an organization that is perfectionist to the core, that glories in content over form, a fair is sure to be instantly ridiculed as the epitome of the superficial. It is self-evident that a fair could never flourish in the atrium of our headquarters—a steel, glass, and marble cathedral that is made for starker things than a carnival. To turn the place into a circus is inconsistent with our history, inconsistent with the cerebral essence of the organization, inconsistent with our prefer-ence for difficult things ahead of visceral pleasures, inconsistent with everything the institution stands for. All this is obvious to me.

Yet my staff persist, and when the knowledge fair duly opens in the spring of 1998, festive lightning strikes. Stiffness and cynicism dis-appear as the organization reveals the sweeter side of its being.

The presidential ceremony opening the fair commends the undertaking with a personal touch of inspiration. Acolytes hover attentively in the vicinity as a cavalcade of senior managers parade by to view the booths. Genial vice-presidents beam proudly in front of professional-looking kiosks housing knowledge-related objects. Passersby stare at a giant glowing poster of rain forests of deepest green. In another booth, photographic enlargements of enormous golden corn sprout forth. Further on, photos of smiling faces of mul-ticolored children in school beguile passersby with their self-evident thirst for education. Next to it, a map of the globe with flickering lights indicates ubiquitous telecommunications links. Plunging charts show the depth to which East Asian countries have sunk in the ongoing financial collapse. Videoconferences with field offices in dis-tant continents underscore the presence of the global village. Exhibits seem to spill out of the booths, as booth sponsors chat happily in front of their displays and extol the advantages of their wares in unusually loud voices, talking with staff ambling by, or going to see what other booths are doing. Energetic aides push brochures under everybody's nose. Swarms of pretty assistants entice clients with a smile to make an impromptu visit to a booth. One setup offers on-the-spot photos with a life-sized replica of our organization's president.

The banners hang long and lovely and sway in a tantalizing fashion. Some booths opt for brash displays of flash and creativity. Others choose a more subdued and demure look, stressing access and solid content, breadth and depth. The fair hovers entertainingly between spectacle and kitsch.

People talk, discuss, negotiate, chat, plan, plot, connive, complain, praise, and everywhere have unexpected encounters. Computer screens go on endlessly with their prepared messages. The atrium is filled with noise. The cacophony is magnified by the shimmering surfaces of glass and marble.

Amid such hyperbolic jollity, it is hard not to be in good humor. Everyone feels bigger, more generous. Nothing is too much trouble. Everyone is constantly praising someone else. No one takes the exaggerations too much too heart. People talk to people they haven't seen for years. Even the most harried staff stop by to check the relevance of content for their next undertaking, and stare mesmerized in front of gaily moving screens. Behind the scenes, technicians struggle with the plugs of computers that have suddenly died. There is vigorous competition to be known as the best booth at the fair, to have the widest sign, the splashiest banner. People are competing for the pure honor of it, not for anything solid. Suspicions of tactics analogous to ballot stuffing ripple through the participants. At first, this irritates, and then entertains, as though a transparently clumsy act of manipulation is consistent with the happy-go-lucky attitude of the thing. Several thousand tote bags with the fair's black-and-gold logo are handed out. Uniformed security guards stroll slowly through the booths, viewing everything and everyone with subdued curiosity.

People are immersed in such a swirling mass of humanity that they enter into the spirit of it and become eager to converse. The organized frivolity forces people to stand around to talk and watch and listen. Instead of the awkward pall that comes over people in the formal meetings, there is a relaxed amiability about the atrium that is practically unnatural. All sorts of haphazard interactions happen. The president rubs shoulders with a secretary. A visitor from Brazil questions her vice president.

The ostensible purpose of the fair is to bring the vision of knowledge sharing down to earth. The fact that the organization orchestrates the chaos makes it okay. It is chaos made manageable and attractive, contained within a frame. People bounce off each other in random motion like so many atoms in a container of gas.

In the process we discover something else—a way to orchestrate and catalyze a massive amount of informal storytelling. Collective events where everyone can tell of their experiences and share the meaning among many. It is a place where people can make connections. Above all, it is occasion where multiple informal storytelling can take place:

- In a conversation with a booth sponsor, a task manager discovers Web sites relevant to her work.

- Another is told about the availability of model bidding documents on line.

- A health specialist hears that a computer model for calculating the burden of health statistics is available.

- A manager discovers the existence of a community of practice in her area of expertise. She signs up so as to receive notices of meetings and newsletters.

The show is so engrossing that people stop just to watch it and discern the plots and subplots. X is talking to Y: what could that be about? It is the perfect world in which to tell stories—anecdotes, examples, narratives, horror stories, war stories, highlights, lowlights, catastrophes, and near misses—a cornucopia of storytelling. Fragmentary intermittent conversations seem more significant than sustained ones. Thousands of informal storytellings in a short space of time, one on one, eyeball to eyeball. People can see meaning and relate it to themselves.[3]

*OWNERSHIP: MASTERING THE PERFORMANCE SPACE CAN HELP IN FORMAL STORYTELLING WITH THE MOST DIFFICULT AUDIENCES.*

The knowledge fair is at the opposite end of the spectrum from formal storytelling. A fair entails the telling of many stories to convince single individuals in unpredictable combinations. A formal performance, by contrast, involves a single telling that must convince many. It is high risk and high profile and hence needs careful preparation. One of the most difficult and pivotal of the formal presentations was the one I made back in February 1997 with the groups of managers who had been formally instructed to attend.[4]

I can see now how important the storytelling performance itself has been in eliciting change. Without a performance, the story never registers or resonates. With no story, there is no communication, no energizing, no change idea, and ultimately no change. The foundation for a good storytelling performance lies in securing the performance space as one's own.

Some presenters will send an assistant to book the room, or check out the audiovisual equipment, or the lighting, or the seating—or worse, not even bother to check in advance at all—because this is menial work and not fit for a presenter's attention. This is often a fatal mistake. In the first place, the assistant will often get it wrong, not because the assistant isn't trying or isn't competent, but simply because an assistant cannot know what the presenter intends. Only the presenter can know that. And there is no way that the presenter can tell the assistant in advance, since the presenter often doesn't know either, until arriving and seeing the physical arrangements and how they relate to the proposed presentation.

---

[3] See on the importance of spectacle in the Italian marketplace: Luigi Barzini, *The Italians*. London: Hamish Hamilton, 1964.

[4] Discussed in Chapter 2.

In February 1997, in the case of the Chile story[5], so much is hanging in the balance for me that there is no risk of making this mistake. I need to see for myself. And so my efforts to secure the space for the presentation begin at least a week before the appointed day.

At that time, I inquire to find out which room has been assigned. On ascertaining the location, I call the technician who is responsible for running the audiovisual facilities and am assured that everything is impeccable. He tells me that the room enjoys the very latest in projectors, and that there is no need to see it since the equipment is built-in. Everything that I can possibly need is already there.

I reply that this is surely so, but I would, in any event, like to try it. I am told that this will not be possible, since the room is being used every day for an ongoing meeting. He says that there is no alternative but to forego the rehearsal. And besides, there have not been any problems before.

The discussion with the technician at this point becomes heated, as I insist on seeing and testing the performance space, and he maintains that there is no real need. I persist, and eventually get him to concede that a test is indeed feasible: the ongoing meeting in the room cannot go on all night, and we will be able to find a time. We set a time late at night when we can inspect the room and see whether it will be suitable for the purpose that I have in mind.

When I go to the presentation room at the appointed hour, the technician lets me in to what turns out to be a medium-sized L-shaped room. The technician was correct when he said that there is a projector built into the ceiling. There is just one problem, and it is a big one. The projector is facing a screen at the end of the foot of the L, with a pillar constructed in such a place that at least half of the audience in the room will be unable to see the screen. How such a decision could have been taken—to build in a projector pointing to a screen that is visible to only half of the room—is a mystery.

---

5 Discussed in Chapter 2.

The next day, I ask the organizers of the meetings whether we can get another room. The answer is that we can't. The reason offered is that we have three groups of managers who are being exposed to three successive presentations on the major changes under way in the organization—one on budget, one on personnel, and the final one, mine, on knowledge sharing. It is essential that the three presentations take place in adjacent spaces, and hence there is no possibility of changing the space that has already been designated.

I can see that if the room can't be changed, then the projection arrangements will have to be. We establish that a white board at the foot of the L would serve very well as a projection screen and can be seen by everyone in the room, provided that we can provide our own projector. At this time—February 1997—projectors that work reliably with laptop computers are not widely available in our organization. My own unit doesn't have one. I have to beg a friend in another section to lend me a projector.

We then try it out, yet again after hours. There is no need, I am assured by the technician, since it is certain to work. After my earlier experience, I am leery. Until I can see for myself, I won't be able to relax.

This time, as it turns out, my anxiety is unjustified. Yes, the projector works perfectly. In the process, I became familiar with the lighting, the dimmer, the switches, and their idiosyncrasies. I run through the presentation and look at the finest print of the slides from the back of the room, and make sure that everything is legible. I check that between the projector and my laptop computer, the colors don't shift as a result of the interaction. On this occasion, nothing untoward occurs, but in the process I develop some expertise with the projector, the setup, and the light switches, as well as how to recover if anything goes amiss.

Is all this trouble and fussing over logistics and performance really necessary? My answer to this question is that if we take care of the basics, and master the performance, we will be ready when the moment of the performance comes, and so be able to cope with the kind of jittery excitement that a newly licensed pilot might feel as his plane is accelerating down the runway to take off for the first solo flight. Instead of transmitting an image of hesitant and flustered bumbling with projectors and computer connections and light switches and screens, instead of wasting precious attention on any of the inanimate aspects of the performance, we can give our all to telling the story for the listeners.

The performance space thus needs to be mastered, so that we can focus all our conscious attention on the human interactions, on telling the story, not on the inanimate logistics. Knowing is not thinking: knowing begins when thinking ceases, having finished its work. It is in this sense that we must know the performance space where we are going to make the presentation, having left behind the necessity to think about how to get the mere logistics to work. When we reach this level of understanding, we know instinctively where the light switch is. We know where the device to change slides is. We reach for it smoothly, effortlessly, unconsciously. We cease to be aware of the physical space. All our attention is on the listeners. The learning process is over. We are masters of the space.

How does this mastery happen? We humans own space by embracing it in our minds. When we have fully incorporated the space into our minds, our minds enfold the space, as if there is no separation between us and the space. Everything is included in our mind, so that we are the space. We are not there simply as one individual disconnected from the room. We are the room. We have security in our feeling. Our mind does not expect anything from outside. It is already filled. If the lights fail, we are not surprised. We take it in our stride. It is an insignificant ripple on the surface of our minds. We amplify the mind so that it embraces the entire space.

The key ingredient in storytelling is oneself—what one brings to it, the feelings and emotional commitment. If one relaxes and lets one's character shine through, this will be more important than all the tips and guides that one can find in the world. Immersing oneself in the story is central to success. The storyteller must feel the story, smell the story, breathe the story. Mentally, we must be there with the protagonist. We must be intensely living the story, being mentally present with the health worker in Zambia, with the task team when they met with the client in Chile or Yemen. We cannot feel the story with this level of intensity if we are worrying about logistical difficulties, about details of the room, whether the projector will work, how to move from one slide to another, or what has gone wrong with the light switches. If we can master these logistical issues and put them out of our mind so that we can feel the story strongly and deeply, then the audience may also feel it deeply, and then we are on the way to telling a successful story.

*TESTING: IT IS NOT VOLUME OR QUANTITY THAT STIRS ANY GROUP. IT IS INTEREST AND MEANING.*

Given the huge number of variables involved, and the necessarily limited information about them, there is typically no way to predict the impact of a story on a particular audience in a large organization except by trying it out and seeing what happens.

One further stroke of luck for the presentation in February 1997 was that I had a chance for multiple rehearsals on live audiences. A large retreat of staff was being held, just prior to these three presentations for the managers. At the retreat, I was provided a room that served as a kind of a booth. The idea was that participants at the retreat could wander into the room based on interest, and we could run the presentation. People could come and go as they liked. As a result, I had the opportunity to try out the presentation on successive audiences and I could test several variants, ultimately going through the full presentation about five or six times. The informal setting permitted free-flowing interaction, with an opportunity to judge the listeners' interest and make adjustments to the presentation to align it with my style. In the process, I became intimately familiar with the interaction between the words and the visuals as well as the impact on listeners of telling the story differently.

Each time I would tell the story of Chile, I got to know the story better, as though I were living it afresh. Each time, I found myself telling it a little differently, as the elements presented themselves slightly differently to my thinking, and I adjusted them in small ways to the body language of the listeners. As a result, each time the story meant something a little different. It was not that I was learning the story by rote as a result of these multiple rehearsals. It was rather that I got used to adjusting the story to fit each particular group of listeners, making tiny variations and adjustments as required.

The result is that I can never perfect a definitive telling for the story. Each time I tell it, I feel as though I have only a partial grip on the sequence of events and their implications. I hold them for no more than a moment in my mind as they slip through my lips. Each separate version of the story is not simply a remembrance of what I was thinking the time before, but rather a fresh rendition. At first, the divergences make me nervous, but eventually I sense that they do not constitute a problem that needs to be resolved. Rather, they are central to the telling—a part of the never-ending effort to generate freshness of perception. As storyteller, I find myself reliving the story and saying each time what I see and feel. With each telling, I seem to see and feel things slightly differently, and in the process, I generate spontaneity of expression. My experience in becoming comfortable with these multiple, subtly different versions of the story develops my competence in telling that particular story. When I get to the morning of the main performances, I am mentally ready for anything.

Experimenting is best done initially in small groups, or even on a one-to-one basis, where the reaction to both the overall thrust and the smallest details will be immediately apparent. In this intimate setting, one can see instantly whether the listeners are opening up to other possibilities in the initial ice-breaking segment, whether they get the point of the springboard story so that the central idea emerges in their minds as their own idea, and whether they are seeing the change idea in the right light. With an individual or small group, one can easily explore modifying the springboard story and see whether the modification has the intended effect. Also, in a small group, or individual presentation, the downside risk of an adverse reaction is much lower than in presenting the idea to a large group.

If the springboard story is to generate a new input to the organization life story, it must operate at a deep level of belief. The storyteller helps the listeners reach this deep level by conveying the special import that this particular story has. The telling of the story must convey the feeling that the events no longer have their simple significance, but instead are invested with a special level of meaning, a prejudice for things essential to express the underlying idea. Through the story, and the way in which it is told, the storyteller makes a special and particular vision clear.

So the springboard story is not fundamentally a story about Zambia or Chile or Yemen at all, but rather a story concerning the deeper meaning of the way the world is—or could be—ordered. The storyteller must feel this in the first place, and feel it intensely; otherwise the audience will never see it or feel it. The deep feelings of the storyteller will seep into the story, and from there into the minds of the listeners, and so help take the audience to the level where deep meaning resides.

# TEN

# Building the Springboard Story

*The truth knocks on the door and you say, "Go away, I'm looking for the truth," and so it goes away. Puzzling.*

Robert Pirsig, *Zen and the Art of Motorcycle Maintenance*[1]

"**W**as it the fonts?" asks one.

"It must have been the colors," says another.

"I think that it was the transitions," says a third.

The group of managers that I am overhearing has just been watching a presentation of mine on knowledge management, with a mixture of wipes and fly-ins—between and within the slides projected onto a large screen. "It was the transitions that gave the whole presentation a sense of flow and movement."

"But the examples?" says a fourth. "Wasn't it the examples illustrating the analysis that gave it the impact?"

As I listen to this conversation, I am packing up my laptop, uncoupling the connection to the projector, and winding the power cord around the power adapter. The group of managers who invited me to come and make the presentation is standing no more than fifteen feet away from me and discussing among themselves the presentation that they had just seen, comparing it to a presentation that they

---

[1] Robert B. Pirsig, *Zen and the Art of Motorcycle Maintenance: An Inquiry into Values.* New York, Morrow, 1974, p. 5.

themselves are preparing on a similar topic. "What was it," they are asking, "that gave the presentation its impact?"

I listen to the conversation flow back and forth. Finally, the conversation ends without coming to a conclusion, and one of their number is sent to request my help. Would it be possible, he asks, for me to take the slides of a presentation that they are working on and jazz them up, so that they will have the same effect as mine just had? "Do whatever you would do so that the presentation will have the same impact?"

As it happens, I have already seen the slides that they are preparing and know that they contain only tangled masses of analytic abstractions. *Do whatever I would do?* With such a mandate, I have a chance to impart some of my art. I immediately set my mind to list the possibilities to adjust the structure of the presentation.

I consider four main options.

> *A. IMMEDIACY: LAUNCHING INTO A STORY AT THE OUTSET HAS PROVED EFFECTIVE, EVEN WHEN IT ISN'T A DIRECT ANSWER TO THE QUESTION THAT HAD BEEN POSED.*

The most effective course of action, the course that I have been pursuing, without exception since my delivery of the Yemen story in late 1997, is to launch into a story at the outset of the presentation, so that the listener sees everything else in the presentation through the prism of the living story. From inside the idea of the story, the listeners can see everything constructively, creatively and generously filling in the missing links. As partners in the idea with the presenter, they can join in bringing the idea to life, since they are listening to everything as participants.

By contrast, if one begins with analysis, there is a risk that the listeners will approach everything with sharp pencils, with unforgiving minds, drawing crisp distinctions and sharp angles, demanding Euclidean precision from imprecise phenomena. They will listen to the words as critics, discerning the presentation as observers, as if watching the spectacle in a detached, dispassionate, hard-hearted fashion.

When I begin a presentation with a story, there are usually one or two slides merely to remind people what general subject we are talking about, that is to say, the overall idea of sharing knowledge. And then without further ado, I launch into the story or stories.

My underlying assumption is that I am dealing with audiences who are ready to listen to what I have to say and that I have their attention at least for the opening seconds. In my case, this has been so since 1997 when knowledge management has acquired official acceptance as a central organizational strategy. At a minimum, knowledge sharing has become something with which everyone had to reckon and cope with in some measure.

When I have the audience's attention at the outset, I find that launching into the story as early as possible in the presentation helps draw the audience inside the story and hence inside the idea that the story embodies. The listeners can then start to see the idea, not as a voyeur, but rather as vicarious participants who live the story, however briefly, and who might, if the story is well told, put themselves in the shoes of the protagonist, undergo the experience of the protagonist vicariously, and feel the feelings of the protagonist—and then, silently, mentally, almost unwittingly, start to build a second set of comparable stories in relation to their own context, their own experience, their own vocabulary.

I have followed this practice even where the purported reason for the presentation appears on the surface to be less than directly relevant to storytelling. When, for instance, I am called upon to make a status report on knowledge management for the very senior people in the organization, I begin with a story, and only later move on to report on the program's status.

I do not ignore the requested purpose of the presentation willingly or easily, since my initial reflexes, instilled in me by decades of education in the analytical method, tell me to begin the presentation by responding to the question that had been asked. This would mean first defining the subject and analyzing the status of implementation on knowledge sharing and only later launching into some stories to illustrate. In fact, in late 1998, when called upon to give a status report, my first draft of a high-profile presentation adopts this more traditional pattern. Fortunately, a colleague advises me during a dry run of the presentation that I am being naïve and convinces me to begin with the story. He persuades me that if I begin the presentation with analysis, this will lead directly into a discussion whether the analysis of the situation is accurate. There will be a tendency on the part of the audience to become critical and adversarial, falling instinctively into the role of stern external observers and judges of the status of sharing knowledge, quick to find flaws, and slow to sense potential.

With a program such as knowledge management that is aimed at transforming an organization, and that is in the full swing of implementation, the status of the program is inevitably that of a glass that is neither totally full nor completely empty, but somewhere in between. In such a situation, the audience could either focus on the glass being partially full (and on how to make it fuller) or focus on it being partially empty (and on why it is so empty). The effect of beginning the presentation with the analysis of the status of implementation is to run the risk that the audience will dwell critically and skeptically on all the program's flaws and blemishes, rather than dwelling constructively on how to remedy the difficulties of implementation and fill the glass to the brim.

And so I switch around the order of the presentation, launching immediately into two springboard stories, and only then going through the analytical material on the status of implementation and the problems that implementation is facing. One of the stories that I use is in the area of decentralization.

> *In March 1998, the Government of Zambia had announced that it was planning to introduce elections for the mayors of its cities—previously mayors had been designated by the president of the republic—and*

*was grappling with the question of how to implement the mechanics of the decision in terms of organizing mayoral elections. The field office of our organization alerted the task manager of public sector management of the ongoing discussion within the Government of Zambia and inquired whether we had any expertise to help.*

*When we consulted our existing knowledge base in the area, there was no relevant guidance and so the task manager contacted, by electronic mail, the community of experts in the subject area, inside and outside our organization, and asked for help.*

*And help arrived promptly. An expert from one unit contributed the experience of Madagascar, which was closely analogous to the situation of Zambia. An adviser from the urban community of experts contributed a set of insights stemming from the thought that the question had been framed in the wrong way: it wasn't so much an issue of how to organize the mayoral elections themselves, but rather how to harmonize the elections of both the mayors and the city councils so that ongoing power struggles didn't dominate the political agenda. And several experts from outside organizations also chipped in with their contributions.*

*As a result, the task manager, instead of being unable to make a contribution to the problems, was in a position to provide a broad spectrum of advice from around the world, just enough and just in time.*

The story is a long way from being universal, or even typical, of the status of the implementation of knowledge management in our organization at this time. Not all task managers are doing what the task manager in this instance did—that is, broadcasting her ignorance on a subject central to her ostensible expertise to a large number of colleagues and asking for help. To do this in an organization such as ours that is downsizing is perceived by all but the most secure employees as entailing considerable risk. And not all the communities of experts are as helpful and responsive as this one turned out to be. But once I have told the story of the task manager providing advice on how to organize mayoral elections in Zambia, I can relate the subsequent analysis of the constraints on expanding knowledge sharing to the specifics of this particular case. Instead of talking in general terms of task managers not drawing on the resources of the communities of practice, I can talk about the situation of the task manager for Zambia, and people can see immediately why there might be hesitation on her part to say, "I don't know." Instead of the discussion degenerating into generalizations about staff resistance to change, there is a natural momentum toward seeing how one can empower task managers to feel emboldened to act as the task manager in Zambia did.

In other words, by beginning the presentation with springboard stories that are explicitly admitted to be atypical, the ensuing discussion inevitably develops into a positively oriented debate as to how to change the organizational constraints so that they will become typical.

Once the listeners have entered the portals of the story, I can then proceed to the analysis and explanations of what is happening, the challenges that remain to be addressed, and the practical insights on what needs to be done next. In this way, the storytelling is the structure, and analytical scaffolding adds support to it. The stories are not mere examples of the analysis; rather, the analysis is an extrapolation of the story to guide the understanding of the narrative. I thus build the analysis and identification of patterns on the basis of the story that is told up front. The stories don't merely illustrate the message—they are the message. The analytical propositions illustrate that message and expand its amplitude.

It is not that the analysis needs to be removed from presentations, but rather that it needs to be integrated in, and subordinated to, the story. The analysis should build on the story, be related to the story, and flow from the story. In this way, we experience the analysis from inside as a participant immersed in it, rather than as a kind of voyeur, looking in from the outside, with curiosity or enmity but little empathy.

*B. SERENDIPITY: WHEN WE AREN'T TOO SURE OF THE FOLLOW-UP ACTIONS, THE TELLING OF MULTIPLE STORIES CAN HELP ENHANCE THE CHANCES OF THE AUDIENCE CO-CREATING THE FOLLOW-UP.*

A second approach is to tell a series of stories. This is what I did in February 1997 when I told a series of stories, starting with the Chile story, and presented them like a string of railway carriages, illustrating how the change idea of sharing knowledge was being implemented.

I did this largely because we didn't know what else to do. At this time, we didn't really know how to go about implementing the details of knowledge sharing. There was no budget in place. There were no agreed operational programs. There were no clear organizational responsibilities. And the knowledge communities that we would later come to see as essential were still little more than an inchoate suspicion. Knowledge partnerships were far off in the future. No one had even mentioned the possibility of building knowledge sharing into the performance evaluation system. We had opinions about these things, but nothing specific had been decided.

In other words, we couldn't present the details of these elements that would end up being crucial for implementation, because we didn't yet know what they were.

In retrospect, one option would have been for me to make them up and present a detailed blueprint for the organization to implement.

The alternative was to let the audience create the details. Plant the seed of the idea of knowledge sharing, and let them invent the missing elements. So we told stories and let the audience imagine for themselves what it might be like, in the context of their own work and problems. Since each person's work and problems were different, no presentation could conceivably deal with them all. Instead, what we did was to offer some illustrations of how knowledge sharing was already working in several different contexts—and could, with a little extrapolation, work in the future—and so spark some collaborative and constructive thinking in the audience about how they might make it work for them.

Later on, when budgets and programs and organizational responsibilities and knowledge communities had been decided—that is to say, when we were in a position to be more informative—we tended to rely on one or two well-chosen stories and draw out the implications and the specifics from the story. Earlier on, when the specifics weren't ready, the expedient that we adopted was to let the audience imagine the specifics.

Telling many stories about what happened could thus help the audience by imparting the idea of knowledge sharing, not only to understand the past, but also to envisage and co-create the future. What the stories offered was this essential quality of an understanding of the relatedness of things: how knowledge-sharing activities had meshed together productively in the past, potentially signaling a new form of order in this working world. In all the multiplicity of ideas and devices and actions and things, there was an implicit order in which the internal aspects of the organization's existence were in harmony. Since the understanding of the audience grew seamlessly out of the past, it could flow smoothly into the future. The series of stories provided not only insight into what had happened so far, but also an indication of what would come next.

*C. SENSITIZATION: STARK DELINEATION OF ONGOING PROBLEMS CAN HELP AN UNRECEPTIVE AUDIENCE TO SEE THE RELEVANCE OF A SPRINGBOARD STORY.*

A third approach is to begin by accentuating the problems that the change idea is meant to solve, and then narrate the story as an example of how to solve the problems. This is what I did early in 1996 when there was no consensus that there was even a problem to solve. Practically no one was even aware of the notion of knowledge management, and only a handful showed any explicit interest in the issue. At this time, I was confronting an almost universally unreceptive set of listeners.

With such audiences, I found that launching into an explanation of knowledge management, even with a persuasive story, was likely to turn people off from the moment I mentioned the term. They simply weren't interested or ready to hear about the idea. I found that it was even less helpful to say that other organizations were getting very interested in this issue. "Knowledge management" was seen as a jargon term, low in cognitive content, esoteric at best, and hence generally assumed to be nonsense.

I therefore had to do something different, something that could from the outset arouse a listener's interest, before I could go on to show what sharing knowledge was about. In order to communicate with an audience, I had first to seek out the listeners in their inner world, their life, and environment as they were experiencing it, so that they would begin to listen to what I had to say.[2]

One advantage that I enjoyed was that I knew about the operations of the organization, and I was willing to listen to the concerns of the managers and staff. I was familiar with the issues that were bothering people at the time. I had lived in a similar world for many years, and I knew its joys and frustrations. So the stratagem that I adopted involved focusing on problems that I knew listeners were themselves aware of, and to varying degrees, concerned about.

Thus, I knew that most of the staff were suffering from a simultaneous flood and drought of information. On the one hand, they could never seem to get exactly the specific information they needed at the right time. On the other, they were being inundated with data and information from every conceivable source. This flood-and-drought syndrome was extremely frustrating to everyone. We were all under great time pressure. It was a universally and acutely felt concern. My understanding of this problem offered an entry point into a dialogue with the listeners.

So for the opening of my presentation to generally unreceptive audiences, I set out to describe the flood-and-drought problem more explicitly and starkly than they had ever heard it described before. In effect, I was saying: "You think you have a problem, don't you? Well, in fact you do, but the problem is much bigger and much deeper and

[2] See Konstantin Stanislavsky, *An Actor's Handbook; An Alphabetical Arrangement of Concise Statements on Aspects of Acting* (edited and translated by Elizabeth Reynolds Hapgood). New York: Theatre Arts Books, 1963. Reprint, Methuen London, 1990, p. 38.

more widespread than anything you could have imagined. And it's going to get worse." In this way, I began talking about issues that the listeners were already interested in, and I told them something pertinent—and worrying—about these concerns.

My idea was that by the time they heard the outline of the problem, they would realize that this was not merely a problem facing them as individuals; the entire organization was in danger of grinding to a halt unless something was done about it.

And it wasn't just an internal problem. How did clients feel when they couldn't get the information they needed? If they couldn't get the information they needed, what future did we have as an organization?

Thus I gave an account of the sorry state of our information systems—the huge costs, the long-unresolved problems, all so well and frequently documented. In adopting this line of argument, I was deliberately trying to heighten the audience's anxiety, in order to get them to be willing to participate in finding a solution. I found that their ongoing, low-level unease was not sufficient to get them interested in doing anything about it. I was attempting to augment the apprehension, almost to the verge of alarm, by putting into question the very purpose and existence of the organization to which the audience owed its livelihood. Self-preservation was enough to get people's juices flowing.

We couldn't go on as we were. Something had to give. But what?

Against this background of high anxiety, the audience would be in the right frame of mind to think about a possible solution to the problem.

*The future, I suggest, is going to be very much like today. For example in June 1995, a health worker in Kamana, Zambia, logged on to the Center for Disease Control Web site and got the answer to a question on how to treat malaria.*

*This true story happened not in June 2015, but in June 1995. This was not a rich country: it was Zambia, one of the least developed countries in the world. It was not even the capital of the country: it was six hundred kilometers away. But the most striking aspect of the picture was this: our organization wasn't in it. Our organization did not have its know-how and expertise organized in such a way that someone like the health worker in Zambia could access it. But just imagine if we had!*

If building up the springboard story has done its work, the audience is by now already thinking in its own context and situation of how their situation could be different. They are imagining a parallel story in their own mind, what their world might be like if their know-how and expertise are organized to make them easily and quickly accessible.

In organizations in need of major change, where managers and staff are not really very interested in listening to the change that is proposed, the option of beginning by sharply delineating the familiar issues should normally be available. If there is a need for major change, there must be some deep-seated problems. For example, costs are not going down fast enough, competition is growing, innovation is not happening fast enough, turnover is too rapid, morale is low, or whatever are the problems of the particular organization. By describing these problems more clearly and vividly than the audience has heard before, several advantages can be realized.

One is that the storyteller's rapport with the audience will be reinforced. They will see that you understand their situation at least as well as they do, if not better. You are not a foreigner. You are one of them.

Furthermore, since the audience is unconsciously or intuitively or even explicitly aware of these issues, it experiences anxiety as a result. People don't like anxiety. They *want* the problems to be solved. Reminding them that there are unsolved problems can create the conditions where they begin to be willing to put their mental toes in the water of alternative approaches. That is the object of the first segment of the presentation: get the audience to listen and be ready to consider alternatives.

The final and most important advantage is that the depiction of deep-seated problems can serve to channel the audience's attention toward the springboard story. The springboard story is not the solution to the problems. But it can spark the audience themselves to discover the solution for themselves.

*D. URGENCY: WHERE TIME IS SHORT, THE WHOLE WEIGHT OF THE ARGUMENT MAY BE PLACED ON THE STORY.*

A fourth approach is simply to tell a single story.

This is effective when time is very limited—for instance, when I run into someone in the corridor, or in the elevator, and I get the question: "What is this thing called knowledge management?" Telling a story is often the best response. I might have no more than a few seconds in which to explain the idea.

Thus, in 1996 I would often tell the Zambia story on the spot.

*The best way to explain it is through a story. In June 1995, a health worker in Kamana, Zambia, logged on to the Center for Disease Control Web site and got the answer to a question on how to treat malaria. . . .*

There is a temptation in such situations to fall back on the training of one's schooldays and offer an abstract definition of what the change is about. Such an approach is almost always counterproductive, since a complex evolving idea cannot be adequately captured in a definition. It certainly cannot be grasped by a listener who is unfamiliar with the subject.

In any event, with a major change idea, one is trying to disturb the listeners—wake them from their mental lethargy, upset them and provoke them, and in many cases, turn their lives upside-down. One wants them to see this as a positive thing. There is no way to accomplish this by giving a simple definition. One needs to plant a seed that can in time take root in the listeners' minds and in due course lead them to think that it would be a good idea if they turned their own lives upside-down. The quickest way to plant this seed is through a story.

～

With these thoughts in hand, I go back to the group and say that I will be delighted to help them with their presentation. My first suggestion is that they reorient their slides around a story. The response is frosty.

"We've got to leave the content of the slides as they are," they say, "and focus on changing the colors, fonts, transitions, or adding some clip art."

"But surely," I venture, "the success of my presentation lay in the story. Didn't you say that I should do what I would have done? Surely it would be a good idea to reshape the presentation and build it around a story?"

This, I am told, is not what is wanted. When I persist a little and suggest that it will be more effective to build the presentation around some examples being communicated, the real reason for the hesitation is revealed: the content of the slides has already been blessed by higher management. But in any event, in their view, messing with the structure of the presentation isn't necessary. What they want is a better set of visual images. It is evident that the idea of building their presentation around a story appears to them far-fetched, even though they have experienced just such a phenomenon for themselves.

This isn't the time or the place to explain the reasons for using stories in communications. And so I accommodate their request and quickly add a few color gradations and transitions to their draft slide presentation. They review what I propose and express themselves absolutely satisfied with the changes that I have made.

What is striking to me from this incident is that these highly educated and intelligent people are blind to the pivotal role that the stories have played in the presentation that I have made to them, to the extent that they can hardly see the story at all. To them, the difference in their presentation and mine—of which the essence is storytelling—is invisible.

The phenomenon of our being unable to see plain truth is of course not limited to storytelling. It happens frequently in our lives that we miss something obvious and fundamental that is staring us plainly in the face. We are unwilling to admit the obvious. We reject the advice of our colleagues and friends. We pay experts lots of money to tell us the self-evident. We spend time with therapists to help us to grasp what is apparent to everyone around us. And yet often we still fail to see what is screaming for our attention.

ᔓ

I attend the eventual presentation, which takes place a few days later, and I sit in the back of the room that houses an audience of more than a hundred. The presenter does add a tiny tribute to storytelling by mentioning in the course of the presentation an example of knowledge sharing. But the reference comes towards the end of the presentation, and there is scant reference to the example in the slides that appear on the screen. The visuals are mainly bland abstractions. The implication is crystalline: the abstractions are central, and the example is peripheral. The fact that the example is narrated with little inner conviction, as if the narrator is unfamiliar with the specifics of what he is talking about, does not help.

In all, the presentation is competent and informative. Like most presentations, it confirms the presuppositions and assumptions of the audience. Those who are in favor of the premises being advanced remain so. Those who are skeptical are left unaffected. It is the typical business presentation. It is dry, uninspiring, and lifeless.

# ELEVEN

# Embodying the Idea

*I promise to tell the truth, the whole truth, and nothing but the truth.*

Judicial oath

*What lies beyond the margins of our world often sings to us with the voice of a siren, as if calling us into its embrace. First we listen, then we are lured, finally we are seduced.*

James Cowan, A Mapmaker's Dream: The Meditations of Fra Mauro,<br>Cartographer to the Court of Venice[1]

Then abruptly, the mood turns brutal. In the fall of 1998, the financial world looks as if it has been struck by a hurricane. The once-vaunted economies of the Asian miracle crumble, with millions of the middle class thrust into poverty. Japan is mired in seemingly endless recession. The Russian economy has come unstuck in mid-August, sending overstretched investors reeling. Brazil is teetering on the brink. Europe is struggling with the meaning of the Euro. The dollar and the New York Stock Exchange gyrate wildly. The global financial system, which just a few months ago seemed so robust, now appears to be on the very edge of chaos. Amid premonitions of imminent financial catastrophe, the idea of an international institution dedicated to

---

[1] James Cowan, *A Mapmaker's Dream: The Meditations of Fra Mauro, Cartographer to the Court of Venice.* Boston: Shambala Publications, 1996.

finance and lending, which had recently seemed obsolete, now looms as an obvious and overriding global priority.

This is the scene that awaits me when I return to work after a vacation in the fall of 1998. It is not that anyone is against knowledge management, but rather that the number of big issues that can be addressed at any one time is limited, and there is insufficient time to deal with everything. In this hyperventilating environment, knowledge management risks being considered a distraction and pushed to the sidelines.

Such crises are stress checks for a major organizational change. In trying to transform a large organization, one is explicitly assuming a role that is marginal to the core of the old organization—the organization that is—in order to show the way to the new organization—the organization that is to be. In launching a major change program, one is leaving behind the calm of met expectations, the comfort of an established identity. Instead, one dwells on the threshold between the two organizations—the old and the new—and lives in a state of continuing ambiguity. Opting to become an instigator of change means abandoning the solace of the status quo for a wilderness existence. A crisis can expose the fault line on which the organization is resting.[2]

To traditionalists, the global financial crisis arrives like a calming sigh. An old-style financial imbroglio offers an opportunity to return to our traditional role. With a full-scale emergency on our hands, we are back on familiar and reassuring territory: monetary flows, banking crises, old-fashioned financial management. This is how our organization made its reputation. In the just-concluded fiscal year, there has already been a record amount of lending. The strident calls from outside to lend even more give heart to those who love managing financial transactions and solving big economic problems.

---

[2] Jane Hirshfield, *Nine Gates: Entering the Mind of Poetry.* New York: HarperCollins, 1997, p. 203.

Unthinkably large waves of unregulated money are crashing into the fragile bulwarks of the international financial order, which is ill equipped to sustain such shocks. Each hint of new risk sends fresh financial surges sweeping toward undetermined destinations, futilely seeking safe haven from the very crisis that investors themselves have created. Nightmares of financial debacle dance in fevered managerial brains.

Under such dark fiscal clouds, it is easy to portray knowledge management as an aberration, a detour from our organization's true destiny. Now the organization can get back to being an international money machine, mobilizing funds, putting together transactions to handle the global hemorrhage. Lending can re-emerge, with no apology or subterfuge, to help cope with the imminent cataclysm.

For us, to deal with the crisis, it is a time to find new stories, generate new truths, and so reinforce the new organizational identity. We need an opportunity to make the broadened conception of the organization accessible to all.

The opportunity comes sooner rather than later. Before the organization's annual meeting, the president calls for a status report on knowledge management, and so I cast about for a new story.

I reread the stories developed by the staff, but none are quite right for such a high-profile occasion. In asking around, I hear eventually about an incident that occurred in Pakistan, something to do with a controversy over highway technology. Initially, all I see is an email reporting on the replies received from the highway community of practice in response to a request from our field office in Pakistan for advice on pavement design. It is no more than a lead, but it eventually becomes the most successful story that I ever use.

> Let me give you an example of how knowledge management is working in practice. Just a few weeks ago, on August 20, the government of Pakistan asked our field office in Pakistan for help in the highway sector. They were experiencing widespread pavement failure. The highways were falling apart. They felt they could not afford to maintain

*them. They wanted to try a different technology, a technology that our organization has not supported or recommended in the past. And they wanted our advice within a few days.*

*I think it's fair to say that in the past we would not have been able to respond to this kind of question within this time frame. We would have said we couldn't help, or said to them that this technology was not one that we recommend, or we might have proposed to send a team to Pakistan. The team would look around, write a report, review the report, redraft the report, send the report to the government, and eventually, perhaps three, six, nine months later, provide a response. But by then, it's too late. By then, things have moved on in Pakistan.*

*What actually happened was something quite different. The task team leader in our field office in Pakistan sent an email and contacted the community of highway experts inside and outside the organization (a community that has been put together over time) and asked for help within forty-eight hours. And he got it. The same day the task manager in the highway sector in Jordan replied that, as it happened, Jordan was using this technology with very promising results. The same day, a highway expert in our Argentina office replied and said that he was writing a book on the subject and was able to give the genealogy of the technology over several decades and continents. And shortly after that, the head of the highways authority in South Africa—an outside partner who is a member of the community—chipped in with South Africa's experience with something like the same technology. And New Zealand provided some guidelines that it had developed for the use of the technology. And so the task manager in Pakistan was able to go back to the Pakistan government and say: this is the best that we as an organization can put together on this subject, and then the dialogue can start as to how to adapt that experience elsewhere to Pakistan's situation.*

*And now that we have realized that we as an organization know something about a subject we didn't realize we knew anything about, now we can incorporate what we have learned in our knowledge base so that any staff in the organization anywhere at any time can tap into it. And the vision is that we can make this available externally through the World Wide Web, so that anyone in the world will be able to log on and get answers to questions like this on which we have some know-how, as well as on any of the other myriad subjects on which we have managed to assemble some expertise.*

The presentation uses the Pakistan story as an introduction to the status of implementation of knowledge sharing. It explains that the Pakistan example is still not typical. We are in the midst of a culture shift. For the shift to be fully successful, we will need a huge new effort. The management will have to carry the standard.

The reception of the presentation is generous—much better than expected. The management commits to doing what is necessary. The board of directors will be informed. We will explain it to the entire management cadre. Every management team will present it in turn to their staff. A press conference will be given at the annual meeting. A knowledge month will be organized. And so on. Knowledge once again emerges in the foreground. The general predictions of doom and gloom that precede the meeting are dispelled, and we emerge with the future all before us. The presentation leads not to any setback for knowledge management, but to an explosion of new energy and momentum. The global financial crisis is perceived as manageable, particularly if knowledge resources are shared. We are back on track.

⏝

Who could object to the Pakistan example? Who could find fault with it? With such a reception, my own feelings are those of humility and gratitude in the presence of such power. Its impact is little short of miraculous. And therein lies the problem. Such an impact generates its own kind of suspicions and discontent. I encounter begrudging reactions from three different sources. One comes from a traditionalist within our organization, a second from a cognitive scientist, and a third from a professional storyteller.

For traditionalists within our organization, there is puzzlement at the impact of the Pakistan presentation. Issues that seemed massive just days ago now simply evaporate. Instead of my status report sparking the expected court martial as to what has gone wrong with knowledge management, there is renewed energy to press ahead with implementation.

The first guess is that the presentation is too positive, but on closer inspection, it is difficult to object to anything specific. No detail of the current status is misstated. The Pakistan story is explicitly depicted in the presentation as something atypical, the ideal to which we aspire, not the norm that occurs on an everyday basis. The strength of the presentation rests less on the particulars, and more on a fueling of a common mood, a vision of hope surging through the vehicle of a story. The presentation unleashes a dream of a new kind of organization, and it is difficult to take issue with a dream.

The presentation thus does not stint in its depiction of the difficulties that lie ahead. But with the fire lit by the Pakistan story resonating in everyone's minds, interest shifts inevitably to how to resolve the issues. From a vantage point within the story, the flaws of implementation, which are legion, are viewed as problems to be solved, rather than shortfalls in performance.

One traditionalist, a senior manager, harbors the suspicion that the effect of the presentation is linked to the Pakistan story itself. And so the thought occurs that if the Pakistan example can be deconstructed, the shift in mood can be undone. There is an abrupt effort to tear it apart, to find out what was inside it, and so shake off the spell that it has helped place over the organization.

So in December 1998, after a repeat of the presentation for a senior management committee just prior to the organization's annual strategy forum where fundamental budget issues are to be discussed, the manager sends me an electronic message posing some questions about the Pakistan story. "Why," he asks, "did the information have to be delivered to Pakistan with such a tight constraint? Is our organization currently engaged in highways lending there? If it had been, surely the project preparation would have provided the advice needed for Pakistan to deal with its potholes? Wouldn't it make more sense to focus our efforts on the traditional task of improving the quality of projects financed by our organization?" The subtext of his message is clear. Why not go back to the traditional business of our organization—lending. The context for posing the questions is also clear. At the upcoming strategic forum next month, the possibility of shifting knowledge management budgets back to traditional categories will come up. If the Pakistan story can be neutralized, major changes can be made.

My reply is unbending.

Is there a link in the Pakistan example to lending? The manager has surmised that this is a case where our organization is not currently engaged in highways lending (or else the project would have provided the advice needed for Pakistan to deal with its highway maintenance problems). The implication is that this is not a prototypical situation of the organization's business. If this argument can be made to stick, then the Pakistan example can be shown to be an aberration, something that is not central to the organization's future. But the manager's surmise is incorrect. A road sector loan *is* being prepared. The advice is used to design the project financed by the loan and decide on the type of rehabilitation to be financed. But the normal course of project preparation did not, as it happens, generate by itself the answer to the question that emerged unexpectedly in the course of preparation. The attempt to dismiss the example as peripheral fails.

"Why was the client in such a rush? Why," asks the manager, "did the information have to be delivered in a matter of days?" The implication in the question is that the request is unreasonable and not something that our organization should gear up to respond to. The simple answer is that the client, for reasons of its own, was intent on making a policy decision the succeeding week. So the team in Pakistan felt under great pressure to deliver something to the client right away. It was the team that set the forty-eight-hour deadline to focus the attention of the community of practice. The task team did get responses the same day from the highway experts working in Jordan and in Argentina, although it took some days for the advice to come in from South Africa and New Zealand.

To understand how and why the issue arose so abruptly requires a little bit of background. The issue of pavement design is a central question in highway construction. Yet it is an aspect of road engineering on which even specialists have different opinions. There are a lot of guide-based design procedures—almost like indigenous cookbooks. Very often, what works in one environment does not work in another. Pavements contribute a major cost to the road project, and a wide range of options is available at a wide range of prices—sometimes for apparently similar solutions to carry the same load. Pavements simply don't follow the rule that the more money you put in them, the better they perform—you can get a bad mixture of costly materials or a good mixture of inexpensive materials. Pakistan's loading conditions—both environmental and traffic—are very challenging. The issue of what type of pavement to use is important because once decided, the pavement type becomes national policy and is very difficult to change, as huge construction industry and suppliers' interests are at stake. If you do manage to change the approach, it then takes a long time for the local construction industry to catch up. The result is poor quality, procurement inequity, and underdeveloped local industries. There are different agencies subscribing to different pavement design approaches. There are many advantages to standardization—provided that the standards are right.

As to why the client was in such a rush in this particular case, the reasons are bound up in the dynamic of what is happening in Pakistan. Just prior to our organization receiving the request for advice, there had been a change in the leadership of the highway authority. A new chairman had just been appointed as part of the government's overall political agenda to reform the highway authority and implement projects at a breakneck speed to make up for its past performance, which was perceived as dismal.

The new chairman, on taking office, had announced that the national highway authority was making very expensive roads and should make cheaper and more cost-effective roads like the provincial agencies, as they carried the same traffic. His idea was apparently that the national highway authority should adopt a different technology. One interpretation by the staff of the national highway authority was that he was thinking of using an older technology known as water-based macadam technology used in some provinces. Another possibility was that he could be persuaded to introduce a related technology known as inverted pavement technology, which was being explored in other tropical countries with promising results.

The chairman proposed to make a policy decision on pavement design methods and procedures on all new federal roads. He had asked the concerned ministry officials to present him with recommendations within a week. The decision was important because if they opted for a different kind of pavement design—be it water-bound macadam or inverted pavement technology—it could affect the course of highway construction in Pakistan for years to come.

The matter was thus urgent because of the possibility of an imminent policy decision by the new chairman. There was a risk of making the wrong decision, as well as a window of opportunity to get a better policy decision made: if the chairman got the right advice and made the right decision, he could assist in pushing a good policy through the higher-level decision-making process, and then on to implementation at a rapid pace.

The task manager was called upon by his project team counterparts in the national highway authority, who were apprehensive that, among other things, use of water-bound macadam technology across the board would be inefficient and not the right move in terms of policy. By contrast, a decision in favor of inverted pavement technology could be quite promising, but also carried risks. The client request for advice from our organization flowed from the local debate about what kind of policy decision should be taken for roads and pavements in Pakistan. The concern of our field staff was not that any particular technology was an inherently bad idea, but rather than it had application in specific contexts, rather than generally.

As a result of getting advice from Jordan and Argentina the same day, and from South Africa and New Zealand shortly afterwards, the task manager in our field office was able within a few days from receiving the request to help the team in the national highway authority convince the chairman and the ministry that the current roads constructed with water-bound macadam should be studied and a specific note on design and use of the appropriate technology on the national highway network be developed after proper study and consultation.

The availability of the relevant international experience in a timely fashion thus enabled the decision-making to be put on a reasoned and substantive basis, rather than being based on an impression that the current approach of the national highway authority was all wrong or on the illusion that there was a simple silver-bullet solution that would solve everything.

By contrast, if the government had gone ahead in finalizing the wrong pavement design methodology, many years of effort might have been involved in trying to undo the decision and get a better policy decision. We would then have to confront issues such as the government's hesitancy to change an existing national policy. They would ask why our organization had not raised an issue in the first place—having known about it at the time of policy formulation.

There were thus valid reasons why the client needed advice urgently and why an ability to give such advice could have a critical impact on highway administration for years to come. Again, the argument—to show that the client had no valid reasons to be in such a rush—failed.

In any event, the phenomenon of our clients being no longer willing to go along with our organization's traditional sequence of doing things—organizing a mission, sending the mission, visiting the country, writing a draft report, reviewing the draft report, finalizing the report, sending the report, discussing the report—is one that most global organizations are finding. Increasingly, clients want answers now, not tomorrow, and they want the best that the organization can provide. If that isn't possible, then they go elsewhere for help.

Clearly, there was a lot more going on in Pakistan than I revealed in my presentation. Yet ransacking the files for more background and deconstructing the story doesn't undermine its impact for knowledge sharing, which is not so much in the story itself as in the ideas that the story can generate.

It is true that I had not told the audience the whole truth. But no single story can ever tell the whole truth. Trying to find the whole truth about a story is an illusion. As with maps, so with stories. Partial description is built into the very nature of storytelling. No single story can ever reveal everything. The story is necessarily a selection, and the extent of the partial representation depends on the angle of vision. Understanding the angle of vision of a story is a key to understanding it as a representation of reality. The angle of vision also determines the impact that the story has for a particular audience. Any individual story is thus but one of an indefinitely large number of stories that might be told about the same data. Any situation might be the subject of different stories, all of which are incomplete or inaccurate in different ways.[3]

In this case, knowing more about what actually happened in Pakistan does not change the story's meaning, or deflect the effect that it engenders. The manager's efforts to deconstruct the story or to find its meaning are akin to the efforts of a child dismantling a clock in a futile search to find the time inside. The more one learns about the underlying story of Pakistan, the further one is from learning how the example had its impact.

For traditionalists looking at the Pakistan story from an analytical perspective, it is difficult to find the pivot for the shift in mood that it led to. The standard analytical dance—beginning with definitions, followed by premises and evidence, ending with linear infer-

[3] Mark S. Monmonier, *How to Lie with Maps*. Chicago: University of Chicago Press, 1991, p. 2.

ences—is absent. Without this sort of discourse, the masters of
Aristotelian logic see no easy way to insert the sharp point of their
dialectic and exercise the requisite leverage to reverse the momentum.
Accustomed as they are to dealing with hard arguments that satisfy the
intellect alone, they tend to be perplexed when confronted with stories
that generate meaning and feeling and momentum from every sentence, spilling messily from the narrative, florid and evocative. It isn't
anything specific that leads to the change in organizational dynamics,
but more the positive aura created in the audience. Storytelling relin-
quishes a straightforward journey from A to B, and in the end leaves
the listeners suspended on the threshold of reverie.

Storytelling, by drawing on deep-flowing streams of meaning,
and on patterns of primal narratives of which the listeners are barely
aware, catalyzes visions of a different and renewed future. For the traditionalist manager, a smooth and consistent set of syllogisms would
have been less difficult to deal with. The problem for such traditionalists is that the audience response to a story reorders the rules of the
game. Traditional analysts know how to cope with abstractions. They
have little idea of how to combat an unanticipated blaze of the imagination. They lack the necessary equipment to douse the ensuing con-
flagrations.

⌐∽

The traditionalist attack on the Pakistan example is not unexpected. I am more surprised at the adverse reaction of a cognitive scientist when I fly to Boston to discuss with a well-known research
organization the idea of studying how storytelling can contribute to
the learning organization.

On arrival in Boston around lunchtime, we are offered standard
business fare of turkey and tuna sandwiches and Sprite and Diet Coke.
We start discussing, and feeling each other out, mutually probing as to
whether our respective organizations could form a productive alliance.
I explain what our organization does in terms of knowledge manage-

ment. They explain their approach to research on the learning organization. The participants in the discussion are energetic, bright, and sharp. There is electricity in the air. Eventually, I feel comfortable enough to put on the table the idea of doing research on storytelling. I explain my hypothesis that telling a story can in some circumstances be a quicker and more effective way to communicate complicated change ideas. Surely this would benefit from some research to verify or disprove the phenomenon and determine its extent.

To my surprise, my proposal is not welcomed as a promising hypothesis. Instead, I am abruptly accused of being illogical and unscientific. I reply that this is not at all my intent, and I illustrate the power of storytelling. But this does nothing to allay the hostile reaction to the whole idea of doing research on springboard stories.

The most outspoken critic, a cognitive scientist, does not so much discuss the technical merits of my suggestions as attack them. They are revivalist, and Messianic, tantamount to advocating deception. They are also in some way dangerous. By advocating the use of stories rather than analytical reasoning, I am likely, she says, to drag the human race back to the Dark Ages of myth and fable from which science has only recently rescued us.

Initially I am struck by the emotional ferocity of the cognitive scientist's response. She is just as resistant to the idea of storytelling as our own organization was initially to the idea of knowledge management, before I started telling stories.

Her reaction is so strong that I realize the idea of storytelling must in some way be very threatening. It is not merely that she is unwilling to submit it to experimentation. She is unwilling even to discuss the merits of doing so. The suggestion, it seems, is abhorrent in itself. It is as if I have proposed scientific research into the impact of witchcraft or black magic. It will be an unrespectable endeavor for a cognitive scientist, since even studying something can confer on it a status as something worth studying. She seems to be starting from the assumption that storytelling is anti-scientific and almost inherently dishonest, and she is unwilling to revisit the assumption. The fear seems to be that doing research on it will undermine the fabric of abstract reasoning on which she imagines the basis of scientific endeavor rests.

She inquires why I am recommending storytelling in place of logical analysis. How can I recommend these fantastic leaps of logic? How can listeners infer a change proposal from a mere story? Isn't the approach inherently illogical?

I reply that science also rests on similar leaps of logic. When Alexander Fleming noticed in 1928 that the mold in the staphylococcus culture had created a bacteria-free circle around itself, and hypothesized the existence of penicillin, he was making a giant imaginative leap from a single piece of evidence that turned out on further testing to be confirmed. Essentially, this is the same leap of imagination that the narrator of springboard stories is asking of the audience—to make an imaginative leap from a single story and then test whether it is true. This should not be a matter of concern unless one happens to be suffering from the illusion that life or science can be lived in a way that is free of leaps of imagination. It is true that an inductive leap may be more obvious to *ex post* inspection in a short presentation than it is in a scientific generalization that has already been subjected to much testing and analysis. In the case of springboard stories, the evidence may be slender—a single experience of a single person—and the inductive leap may be immense—the future of an organization in the twenty-first century—but the logical structure of the argument is identical to that of science. The question is not whether there is a leap of imagination; the question is whether the right leap of imagination is made—and for this purpose, rational analysis and testing is needed, in organizational change as much as science.

Thus, I am not proposing to replace logical analysis with storytelling, let alone drag the world back into the Dark Ages. I am recommending on the contrary that any change idea should be subjected to the most rigorous and stringent analysis to ensure that it is sound, before any change process is launched. The story does not replace rational analysis, but rather opens up new mental horizons and perspectives, which can then become the subject for analysis and testing. It recommends where appropriate the subtlety and indirection of Plato's dialogues ahead of the clarity and directness of Aristotelian exposition, not because the former is in any sense better than the latter, but rather because the former is more useful in communicating with an unreceptive audience. There is thus no intent to deny the role of logical analysis in rational discourse, even though it is not accorded a monopoly. My suggested approach to communication in fact offers a more important role to logical analysis than the traditional explicit exposition, since it invites the listeners to set aside their prejudices and make up their own minds, rather than trying to communicate a predetermined conclusion.

These arguments do little to mollify her. Her final accusation is that as a storyteller I am guilty of trying to seduce my listeners. I surprise her by conceding there are some analogies between persuading an organization to change and the subtleties of seduction. She responds as though she has registered an intellectual deathblow by obtaining such an admission, evincing the emotional glee akin to that of a prosecutor who has extracted a guilty confession from an accused. We part with no plans to meet again.

As I fly back to Washington in the evening, I ponder the day's events. I had set out in the morning with the specific objective of getting her organization to do research on storytelling. In this respect, the day has been a complete failure.

I can see that the tactics that I have employed on this visit have been utterly ineffective. What went wrong?

One dimension of the failure is that I have come on too strong. Instead of offering a springboard story in which the research scientist would herself discover a new future, I have adopted the Napoleonic approach of a frontal assault using the tools of logic and reasoned argument. By making clear my specific objective from the outset—to change the cognitive scientist's research agenda—I have appeared to threaten some of the underlying assumptions of her life and livelihood. A more indirect approach might have been more effective.

As I fly back to Washington, I realize that I am disappointed with the outcome. I wanted very much to have the endorsement of the cognitive scientist and her organization in order to establish that what I am about has wider acceptance and respectability in the scientific community. It is obvious now that I will have to look elsewhere for this. As I mull over the day's events, I can see that for all my convictions on the powers of feeling and narrative, I am still very much in the grip of the traditional scientific thinking, and was looking forward to getting a blessing. I have not yet shaken free of the mindset that if the cognitive scientist and her organization accept my agenda, it will have validity, and if they don't, then maybe it doesn't. In this way, my effort to interest the scientist and her organization has been connected to a wish to do something about this power over me, to which I have succumbed from the outset. I have to admit that I am still in thrall to these traditional scientific thinkers, and the attempted persuasion has been in some ways an attempt to set myself free.

As I arrive in Washington, I conclude that this has been a very strange encounter. As the admitted trafficker in storytelling and emotion, I have been arguing in a scientific and rational way, while dealing with a cognitive scientist who uses emotional pleas to bolster her refusal to undertake scientific research on the subject.

I had set out to present my case on its substantive merits on the assumption that surely a cognitive scientist would be amenable to an analytic and rational discussion. Instead, I find myself dealing with pleas to sentiment and feeling to make the case for resisting further analysis or research. If only I had had an appropriate springboard story to get her to see things differently! In contrast to logic and analysis, storytelling shyly invites collaboration, and in so doing, gains privileged access to the back door of the mind.[4]

---

4 Jean Baudrillard, *Seduction* (translated by Brian Singer). New York: St. Martin's Press, 1990.

⌐⌐

So much for the traditionalist and the cognitive scientist. What would a professional storyteller say of the Pakistan story? I find out when I travel to a different part of the country—Jonesborough, Tennessee, the home of the National Storytelling Association—to meet with the avowed friends of storytelling. I expect this to be a receptive audience. And on the whole it is. There is great interest in the use of storytelling to enhance organizational performance.

As part of the get-together, I am asked to show the presentation that I make on knowledge management, including stories like the Pakistan example. After the presentation, I ask a professional story-teller what he thinks of the Pakistan story. He is a colorful character with a folksy manner and a vast repertoire of country tales and gags. He is an extraordinary performer.

To my surprise, he says that he didn't hear a story. There was no telling of it. There was no plot. There was no celebration in it. There was no building up of the characters. There was no description of the look of the eye of the client, or the smell of highway construction. As a result, he never got into the story. So this just wasn't storytelling. To him, the Pakistan story, as I told it, was a puny thing, not really a story at all.[5]

This objection gives me pause. In our current culture, we tend to consider the storyteller as someone different. We call the storyteller a raconteur, an entertainer. Perhaps we may consider him as not a very serious fellow. Someone who might make his living by telling stories to children, or perhaps a comedian telling jokes to the patrons of meretricious night-clubs, or, if he is very successful, a talk-show host for insomniacs. Listening to a story is something we do when we want to relax and get some distraction or merriment. We listen to such sto-

---

[5] The question of what is true storytelling is hotly debated among professional storytellers: Carol L. Birch and Melissa A. Heckler (editors), *Who Says?: Essays on Pivotal Issues in Contemporary Storytelling*. Little Rock: August House Publishers, Inc., 1996, p. 9.

ries for the story's sake. In these settings, the story is a story in parentheses. It comes with an explicit announcement: I am going to tell you a story. Tah-dah! We know and feel that we are going to be hearing a story with a capital "s," an experience different from having a conversation, talking, or communicating normally. We enter the story as if through designated portals, as we get ready for a formal performance. We follow the story line and at the end, the punch line of the joke links the expected with the unexpected. We laugh and we know that the Story is over. We then look around to see if it is to be followed by another Story, or if someone else has a Story or if we ourselves can retrieve a similar Story from our grab-bag of jokes and anecdotes so that we can continue in the formal Story-telling mode. If not, we lapse back into normal living and communication which, as it happens, also comprises stories, but this time gossip or stories with a small "s" and no "tah-dah."

The teller of the springboard story is mainly interested in stories with a small "s." He or she is not there to entertain. He has entirely different objectives and mode of operation from the storyteller of stories with a capital "s." He does not want the story to stand out as a story. On the contrary, the less the listeners realize that they are listening to "a story," the better.

Equally, the teller of springboard stories, unlike the teller of Stories for entertainment, does not try to re-create all the details of the context at great length and in intriguing detail. The professional joke-teller delights in immersing the audience in the idiosyncrasies of the situation: all the better to spring the punch line on them. By contrast, the teller of the springboard story doesn't want the reader to get too involved in the details of the story. For if the readers get immersed in the details of the story, then they may never make the next conceptual leap and re-create the change idea—and in the process, their own identities—through the help of the story. For this to happen, the springboard story itself needs to be relatively low-profile and unobtrusive.

A springboard story is thus not something you immerse yourself in. It is not something you want the audience to get interested in for any length of time. It is not even very fascinating in itself—rather it is brief and textureless. It might take place so rapidly that one doesn't notice it as a story. When pointed out, it hardly seems like a story at all. If one is expecting a long, magnificent, and fanciful tale—something like the Scheherazade that lasts a thousand and one nights—one is destined to feel disappointed, even cheated. We are not talking about that kind of a Story—a story for story's sake.

As a teller of the springboard story, I have other aims. The springboard story is a means to an end. The end is to join with the audience and to co-create the future. The springboard story is a conceptual springboard, a launching device aimed at enabling a whole group of people to leap—mentally—higher than they otherwise might, to get beyond mere common sense. If they succeed in leaping higher, it is a success. If they don't, and stay stubbornly grounded in yesterday's reality, in yesterday's assumptions, then it is a failure. The springboard story is stillborn if it doesn't lead to the co-creation of the future—no matter how much it entertains the crowd, no matter much it makes them laugh or cry, no matter how much it generates a whole lot of debate.

Nevertheless, when the springboard story is successful, the teller becomes one with the audience and shares a mutual communication space so that storytelling becomes a truly joint venture in common mental terrain. The speaker effectively becomes the listener as the audience creates its own message.

Thus, there are two sorts of stories. One sort of storyteller has the panache of a Charles Dickens or a Mark Twain. With such writers, the explicit voice of the narrator is so large and generous and conveys so much enthusiasm and gusto for life that the reader is swept along by it, and the stories become as real as life itself. These are maximalist stories, or stories with a capital "s."

The stories I am talking about are stories with a small "s." These are more like the spare stories of Raymond Carver, or the parables of Jesus Christ, or the mini-stories of less than fifty-five words. In this other way, the voice of the storyteller is implicit or even nonexistent, depending on how you want to describe it. The minimalist approach leaves a lot of imaginative space for the reader to fill in the blanks. This approach may be more valuable for practical purposes than the direct, overwhelm-them-with-my-charm-and-gusto approach that I love so much in Dickens and Twain, or in Proust with his subtlety, where the author is everywhere so present and visible that one inevitably ends up thinking about the authors, and their personalities and the way they tell the story, as much as any thoughts that the story itself may generate. These writers come on like gangbusters and don't leave much space for the reader's thoughts, and that's fine as entertainment. But when one is trying to use stories to get people to learn about themselves, a different tactic is needed. These heavy-duty storytellers pick us up by the lapels and force us to look at things in their particular way. It's hard to be neutral about these writers. You love them or you hate them. This is fun, but it can be out of place where one is trying to foster collaboration.

⤳

As listeners probe and poke the Pakistan story, they show that it is mundane, obscure, lacking in true storytelling, and even trite. The traditionalist attacks the underlying facts. The cognitive scientist accuses me of being anti-science. The storyteller assails the approach as falling short of true storytelling. But all these efforts do not detract from its effect.

As a springboard storyteller, I am less interested in the facts of Pakistan, or in scientific analysis, or in professional storytelling, than I am in catalyzing organizational change. From this perspective, the Pakistan story suits my purpose. My goal is to embed a way of looking at the world in the listeners' minds, so as to tighten its grip and deepen its roots and hence induce in their thinking a view of the organization and the world with new planes of order and opportunity. In the process, an understanding of the potential of the change idea—sharing knowledge—can erupt into the collective consciousness, producing a sudden coalescence of vision in the minds of listeners. The provenance of these thoughts—in this instance, the story—is not even very important. The spark that starts the fire is less significant than the conflagration that then takes place.

The Pakistan story enables the listeners to envision what it is like to be part of the future. It beckons them inside as a friend. The benign new understanding that it generates can help them invent new identities, new futures. Those identities and futures are never permanent, but go on living, growing, evolving, developing. Even when a consensus emerges, it is, at best, only temporary. Once there is a consensus, the facts that gave rise to it are not particularly interesting, because they no longer teach us anything new. It is the new patterns of looking at the world that are important. These patterns tug at the line, nagging for attention, asking if we'll be interested in them, and turn out to be the growth points of our understanding.

It is the search for ever-improving understanding that lures us on, inviting us to supersede existing patterns. The search is not a struggle to meet any external criteria of excellence, or objectified goals. It means evolving in accordance with the inner structure of the listeners' own being. It begins in each listener's own head and heart and hands, and then moves outward from there. It does not involve the submission of the self to others, or the assertion of one's self against others. It is sympathetic and respectful of attentiveness to others on their terms. The search interacts with, assimilates, and integrates others.

The observer looks at the change idea as being "out there," as being a fixed and unchanging entity. When the change idea is looked at externally and objectively as a voyeur, every step to implement it is an effort, because the goal is complex, external, distant, foreign.

By contrast, from within a story like the Pakistan example, the listeners can get inside the idea, sensing the implications of it so intensely that the idea can become absorbed into their own identity. The idea is infused into their own spirit, so that they can withstand more ambiguity than normal. Living the story can help break the habit of seeing reality as static, rather than dynamic. It is a process of which they are part, not an entity in opposition to them. Following a story enables the listeners to understand the relation of things that results in underlying harmony. Their predilection for consonance is not an imposition on reality, but a response to it and an extension of it.

# TWELVE

## The Medusa's Stare

*This does not mean that I consider the virtues of weight any less compelling, but simply that I have more to say about lightness.*

Italo Calvino, *Six Memos for the Next Millennium*[1]

*The poet's eye, in a fine frenzy rolling,*
*Doth glance from heaven to earth, from earth to heaven;*
*And as imagination bodies forth*
*The forms of things unknown, the poet's pen*
*Turns them to shapes, and gives to airy nothing*
*A local habitation and a name. . . .*

William Shakespeare, *Midsummer Night's Dream*[2]

It is three years since I began my quest to introduce knowledge management into our organization. Now in 1999, the results are everywhere evident.

At the beginning of the year, the strategic forum of our senior management confirms the central role of knowledge sharing in the future of the organization. For the first time, the mission statement of our organization is formalized and incorporates knowledge sharing as a principal tenet.

---

[1] Italo Calvino, *Six Memos for the Next Millennium* (translated by Patrick Creagh). London: Vintage, 1996.

[2] William Shakespeare, *Midsummer Night's Dream*, V, 1.

In the spring, an external evaluation of the knowledge management program is commissioned and confirms the direction of our knowledge-sharing strategy. The evaluation reinforces knowledge management as a key instrument for the organization to achieve its full potential, by mobilizing global knowledge from inside and outside the organization and applying it to solve local development problems in a timely fashion. In the fall, an external benchmarking selects our organization as a best practice partner in terms of successfully implementing knowledge management.

A survey of key external stakeholders shows that this group of stakeholders already sees the provision of global knowledge as one of the organization's most important functions. Internal surveys also confirm the progress. The staff questionnaire at midyear shows that almost three-quarters of the staff believe that they have access to the knowledge and information needed to do the job. Around two-thirds of the staff report that they are encouraged by their managers to share knowledge and to find new and better ways of doing things.

Thus, much has been accomplished. Yet much remains to be done. Action is needed to refresh the organization's web, so that collections of information and knowledge can be more easily found by users. The work programs and performance of the communities of practice need to be consolidated to ensure that their work is increasingly responsive to demand. Improvements are required in the tools for enabling staff to connect with other staff who are knowledgeable about a subject. Work will also need to proceed on developing collections of knowledge that are easily downloadable. Knowledge sharing needs to be further brought into the work of every staff member, not merely the growing core of enthusiasts. Research and other analytic work need to be more closely integrated into knowledge sharing.

Although we are still a long way from fully realizing the vision of an organization completely integrated around knowledge sharing, we are now entering a different, more mature phase of the change process. In the new phase, the challenges are going to be different—less of pioneering a new frontier and more of surveying and demarcating a known terrain. It is less a matter of slashing our way through an unknown jungle with an essentially unspecified destination, and more a conventional management task of getting from a known point—here—to another known point—there.

In 1996, when we set out on this quest, the organization presented itself as a massive bureaucratic apparatus—budgets, staffing, personnel systems, work programs, technology—that was seemingly set in its ways and unresponsive to our efforts. At that time, we saw ourselves as facing the gargantuan task of moving this massive system of machinery with merely a set of ideas—a collection of airy nothings. It seemed far-fetched, even unrealistic, that the hard reality of such a ponderous and unwieldy structure could be shifted by no more than gauzy thoughts.

Yet now, three years later, the vast bureaucratic structure has in fact been reoriented to incorporate the goals of knowledge management. So much so that knowledge management itself has a significant bureaucratic apparatus of its own—budgets, staff, programs, technology, and the rest. The insubstantial vision of 1996 of a different kind of future for the organization has become a reality that is substantial, hard, and tangible.

Although the willingness to have even attempted such a transformation reflects an inevitable element of intrepidity, it was also born with hope and humility, viewing the people of the organization as a source of novelty and invention that suffers when constrained by too many limits. Storytelling was used to champion freedom, interaction, and organic growth in a multitude of directions, and in so doing, advantage was taken of tools that operate beyond the scope of linear logic. By being as interested in the unknown as in the known, we have learned much.

The evolution has been one of wave, of flow, of ecology—an array of interacting patterns. The patterns were inseparable from the whole, making it difficult to extract specific lessons from the flow. In the process, we have catalyzed more than we have managed. The changes have emerged out of interactions among people, their environment, and their ideas.

In this initial period of change, we saw the organization as a living organism that needed to be tended, nurtured, and encouraged to grow. We had faith in its self-organizing capacity. We endeavored to sense what wasn't obvious, to gather insights at the periphery and let these insights feed the central vision. In trying to launch something very modern, we ended up drawing on the ancient wisdom of story-telling in an effort to spring to a new level of intelligence.

In the period that we are entering, the emphasis will shift. We will need to administer the very things that we have generated. Explosive uncontrolled growth will no longer be tolerable. Now that the goals of knowledge sharing are clearer and modalities more apparent, it will be critical to define and deliver on specific outcomes and measurable impacts. It will be the conventional aspects of man-agement that will matter. We will be as dependent on administration as on inspiration. We will aggressively apply modern management methods to knowledge sharing. Building on the growing optimism that we know where we are going, we will need to become more effi-cient at getting from here to there. To retain budgets and to secure work programs, we will be induced to present knowledge management as following a logical path—a more or less straight line from where we are to the goal.

In this new era, we will be expected to talk of knowledge as some-thing that can be measured (even if not absolutely), something that can be traded for a certain value, something that accountants can put on the balance sheet and track from quarter to quarter—a resource that can be extracted from stores of information, the way a precious mineral is extracted from a rock. Whatever the truth of the matter, we will be pressed to present knowledge as though it is an object.

To cope with these pressures, we will draw on the thinking about intellectual capital. We will learn from the engineering guidebooks on creativity and innovation, and share the designer's love of posing problems and finding solutions. We will be adept advocates of new technology. We will take advantage of modern taxonomical approaches to organizing knowledge, and provide convenient structures in which knowledge sharing can take place, from databases to Web sites to structured conversations. In doing so, we will be providing our owners with a reassuring sense of control, a comforting sense of predictability.

The risks in this new era will thus be different. In the prior era, the danger was that we would fail to mobilize the effort needed to move existing heavy structures. In the new era, as we inherit the boundaries and structures of our own creation, we will need to take care that the lines are not misdrawn, since what is outside the boundaries and the structures may often be more important than what's inside. Ultimately, the boundaries and the structures may inhibit innovation and exclude novel points of view if they become too rigid. We will need to be concerned that the more structured approach will produce diminishing returns as a result of the overhead on designing knowledge, capturing it intentionally, and imposing structures on complex processes. We will need to cope with the risk that, as much as we humans like to create new structures, we also resist submitting to them.

We will also have to deal with the normal forms of incursion that occur when significant quantities of staff and resources are involved. More and more often, men and women will arrive with sharp pencils and big yellow pads and large spreadsheets. The staff of the budget and evaluation departments will pay us close attention. These people will be less interested in stories, and instead will give their attention to measures. "What is the cost–benefit? Tell us how this will be reflected in the corporate scorecard? How can we measure success?" We will thus have to spend less time interacting with the living part of the organization and more time managing the artifacts of the organization.

I will look with equanimity when I see the solemn faces of these accountants and budgeteers who will come to my office. I can foresee that they will be indifferent to the insight that measurement inevitably means evaluating things by the standards of the past. They will be unconcerned that measurement is totally appropriate for stable, predictable, linear activities, but less so when an activity is rapidly mutating. They will be less interested in the next generation of change than in the extrapolation of the present. The idea of swirling new emergent phenomena and phase changes that by definition escape the predictable frame of yesterday's conceptions will be somewhat beyond their ken. Even if they are willing to admit that we do not know enough to predict the future, they will keep hoping that just a little bit more work and analysis will reveal the keys that currently escape their grasp. They will be reluctant to admit that the enterprise in which we are engaged will inevitably evolve unpredictably, like a life form in its own right. It will not respond to diktats, but will appear more like a bacterial culture, unexpectedly swelling here and recoiling there in response to technical, cultural, and economic events. There will be a whole lot of morphing going on. These people will have difficulty in seeing that we cannot measure tomorrow when we don't know what it will involve.

The object of the accountants is an understandable one—the attainment of a well-behaved today, to enclose and imprison this uncertain and emergent world in virtual hoops of certainty, and to preserve themselves from the terrors of the unexpected. The truth that they will seek is not the creative struggle to build a new future. They will want a truth anchored in the illusive security of yesterday. Conditioned by the contradictions of their situation, and by the myths of the existing order, they will be interested in minimizing risk and maximizing predictability.

Although storytelling has gotten us to this point where we own programs and structures, I can also now see that the future is going to be different. I will have to spend more time with these demarcationists and controllers, paying tribute to their preconceptions and objectives. Storytelling will not disappear as we continue to use it to evolve and create the future, but it will be less relevant to the more structured task of administering an ongoing program.

In this story to date, we have been mainly concerned with that aspect of the organization that comprises the active, living participation of individuals. We have been discussing how to use storytelling to build a lively, energetic coalition of forces that sees and creates the future. We have been focusing on those who see themselves as creating that vision. We have been dwelling on the living experience of the individuals who act, think, talk, discuss, chat, joke, complain, dream, agonize, exult together, and collectively make up the organization. This focus will continue.

But in the coming period, we will have to give more, and parallel, attention to the artifacts or things that have been congealed, frozen, or reified as part of the organization's existence—the mission statements, the formal strategies, the programs, the procedures, the processes, the systems, the budgets, the assets, the artifacts of the organization. The lived experience and the artifacts of an organization coexist and interact with each other and collectively comprise the organization.

Storytelling is a tool that gives privileged access to the living part of an organization, and so can be used to elicit decisions to create the artifacts in the first place. It can help the instigator of change at any level deal with the paradox facing the large organizations of our age— that major change is essential, but the organizations themselves often seem almost immovable. It can assist in mobilizing large numbers of managers and employees, in support of changes that will initially seem difficult, upsetting, and strange. Storytelling can thus be used to build substantial artifacts, but it is less suitable as a tool for administering them.

In the beginning, the change ideas that we were pursuing seemed to be so light. Now what we have created feels so heavy. In one sense, this is the measure of our success—that we have turned mere dreams into hard reality. We have created artifacts of our own, just as solid and heavy and intractable as the artifacts against which we had been struggling—that is to say, yesterday's congealed dreams. We have discovered that structures are contingent, pragmatic devices, subservient to the shaping spirit of the imagination. Imagination is the instrument of continuing creativity, a power that inexorably propels us forward into the future, the unknown, building new worlds and structures.

It is as though this process of weightless ideas turning into heavy artifacts is a process of living things being turned into stone, a process of petrification, proceeding at different speeds depending on people and places, but one that spares no aspect of life. The ancient Greeks recognized the phenomenon and—as usual—encapsulated it in a story—the myth of the Medusa.[3]

The Medusa is a face, ringed with serpents, whose very stare turns people to stone. The only hero in the ancient world who is able to cut off the Medusa's head is the young hero Perseus, who flies through the air on winged sandals. In cutting off the Medusa's head, Perseus does not allow himself to gaze upon the face of the Gorgon but only upon her image reflected in his bronze shield. To cut off the Medusa's head without being turned to stone, Perseus supports himself on the very lightest of things, the winds and the clouds, and fixes his gaze upon what can be revealed only by indirect vision, an image caught in a mirror. As for the severed head, Perseus does not abandon it but carries it with him on his travels, concealed in a bag. When his enemies in fresh challenges are about to overcome him, he has only to display it, holding it by its snaky locks, and this bloodstained booty becomes an invincible weapon in the hero's hand. It is a weapon that he uses only in cases of dire necessity, and only against those who deserve the punishment of being turned into stone.

The myth has several mesmerizing hints for the dilemmas of modern management coping with the twin challenges of petrification and transformation.

For one thing, there is the insight that the heaviness of stone and the lightness of creativity have the same parentage. Without structure,

---

3 See the discussion in Calvino.

there is no lightness or creativity, since it is structure that enables creativity. We see examples of this everywhere. In nature, we see the fantastic diversity generated by a few basic structural elements: no more than a hundred varieties of atoms and a couple of primary colors lead to a universe of infinite beauty and diversity. The great human creations, the twelve notes of the musical scale, the twenty-six letters of the alphabet—these fantastic structural inventions have unlocked the enormous creativity of literature and music. Without structure, there is nothing for creativity to get leverage upon.

For another, Perseus deals with the risk of petrification by refusing to look at it directly, which would mean becoming petrified as well. He only deals with it second hand, using a mirror as intermediary. In the same way, one cannot change the existing structures by dealing with them directly, but only by looking away, and coming at them indirectly. Finding the source of light and creativity inside organizations means looking outside the existing structure.

Thirdly, like Perseus, we find that, try as we might, we cannot escape the stone reality of petrification. Perseus takes the reality of petrification with him in the form of the Medusa's head that he carries with him on his travels. He accepts it as his particular burden. It remains with him, and will stay with him, even after he has slain the Medusa. He continues to need it. Thus, Perseus himself resorts to the use of petrification when he has a problem he cannot solve in any other way. When all else fails, he uses the heaviness of structure to disable the enemies of creativity. In other words, there is only so far that one can go with creativity alone. To deal with the real enemies of innovation, in the end, a structural solution may be needed. To be fully successful, we need not only the winged feet of storytelling but also the Medusa's head to create new stony structures where needed.

Thus, the story that I have been telling—the use of storytelling as a tool for catalyzing action and change—is in fact part of a larger story, an evolving process of organizational and societal change where storytelling itself is only one tool among several, and where I am only one actor among many.

I have been striving here to portray the organization as it is. I have tried to avoid succumbing to an attitude of romantic fascination with huge institutions. I have struggled to attain a consistency of fit between the image of the organization as it presents itself, and the actual facts and actions that are apparent. I have tried to avoid conferring on the organization any pearly superlatives that it does not deserve. But inevitably I have told only part of the story by looking at things from a narrower angle—the story of storytelling. The larger story, in which I am also a participant, is another story.

In this larger story, those whose goal is merely that of control will find that storytelling is not a very useful or important tool. For them, the important thing is the accommodation to the preoccupations of today, the effort to maintain conformity to a well-behaved and coordinated yesterday. For the instigators of change, the important thing is the continuing transformation and the creation of tomorrow. For those with a goal of control, the preoccupation will be with the content of what to discourse about, which bits of information to transmit.

For the true instigator of change, whose preoccupation is to cause others to think more, the situation is different. Our fundamental objective is to fight alongside the participants for the best and most productive and most constructive ideas, not to win them over to any particular side. We do not bring any specific non-negotiable objective, but rather aim to stimulate the audience to envisage and create their own future. Change ideas will only have resonance for us if they respond to our own preoccupations, doubts, hopes, and fears. In this process, storytelling offers more than a tool. It is beyond all measures, almost a requirement of being alive. Insofar as it has anything to offer, it generates fresh depth and breadth of perception. It enables us to surmount a humdrum world where everything makes sense and is logical, and get to that realm where deeper meaning is revealed.

When we hear a story that touches us profoundly, our lives are suffused with meaning. As listeners, we have transmitted to us that which matters. Once we make this connection, once a sense of wonder has come upon us, it does not last long, and we inevitably fall back into our daze of everyday living, but with the difference that a radical shift in understanding may have taken place. Through the multiplicity of words and meanings, some of the underlying structure of things has become revealed to us. The connectedness between the self and the universe has been reset. We have sensed the world with our nerve endings bare. The story is something that comes from outside. But the meaning is something that emerges from within. When a story reaches our hearts with deep meaning, it takes hold of us. Once it does so, we can let it go, and yet it remains with us. We do not weary of this experience. Why should we? Once we have had one story, we are already hungry for another. We want more, in case it, too, can transmit the magic of connectedness between ourselves and the universe.[4]

Three years ago I started out with the objective of implementing a specific change idea, an objective that was bounded in time and space, and contained within a dimension of success or failure. Now I can see more clearly that the game I am playing has no spatial or numerical boundaries. The outcome is less related to whether the change idea is in the end accepted, as though I am participating in a game that can be won or lost. The game is much broader and more open-ended. Now winning is as insufficient as it is irrelevant. Instead, the game entails continuing to play, to evolve, to grow.[5]

Whether the change idea triumphs is less important than the quality of the interaction. Living instrumentally to achieve explicit fixed objectives is less important than living moment by moment, day by day, appreciating difficulties as much as success. It is a matter of letting go of the urge to control, and the fear that goes with it—learning that the world has the capacity to organize itself, recognizing that managing includes catalyzing this capacity, as well as sparking, cre-

---

4 See Frederick Franck, *The Zen of Seeing; Seeing/Drawing as Meditation.* New York: Vintage Books, 1973, pp. 120–125.

5 See James P. Carse, *Finite and Infinite Games.* New York: Free Press, 1986.

ating, energizing, unifying, generating emergent truths, celebrating the complexity, the fuzziness and the messiness of living, all the time relishing the sense that almost everything one thinks or knows about the world has turned out to be false.

# APPENDIX 1

# Elements for Developing the Springboard Story

**Some elements for identifying a springboard story**

| Characteristic | Explanation |
|---|---|
| The explicit story should be relatively brief and textureless | The story can be brief and should have only enough texture or detail for the audience to understand it. You do not want the audience getting caught up in the *explicit* story, since the objective is for the audience to discover and co-create their own mental story in their own terms in relation to their own context. You want all the listeners' energy and attention given to joining the dots between the implicit story and their tacit understanding. |
| The story must be intelligible to the specific audience | The audience needs to understand enough about the protagonist and the initial incident for them to be *hooked* by the conflict or problem story. In effect, you should provide no more than is necessary for the audience to understand the story, so that the audience doesn't get lost in the story, but can follow its meaning. |
| The story should be inherently interesting | To capture interest, the *actions* described might be difficult, with a *predicament* that cannot be handled in a routine manner, and some tension between the characters in the story; or *unexpected* |

| | *events* happen in an otherwise normal sequence of occurrences. There should be an element of *strangeness* in the story. |
|---|---|
| The story should spring the listener to a new level of understanding | For the story to achieve this effect, it must epitomize or embody the change idea, almost like a premonition of what the future will be like. For the story to be effective with large numbers of the audience, it must be an easy mental leap from the facts of the springboard story to a new input into the various versions of the organization life story that the members of the audience are carrying in their heads. |
| The story should have a "happy ending" | The story needs to spring the listener out of the typical negative, questioning, skeptical frame of mind, and into a positive attitude of *wanting* to understand the explanation of the change idea. For this to happen, the listener must be in a positive *aha!* frame of mind, and a positive ending is much more likely to achieve this effect. |
| The story should embody the change message | Stories can help persuade people to change if there is an implicit change message that is close to the surface of the explicit story, which the audience can discover on its own and make into its own change message. |
| The change message should be implicit | Clarity is ideal when the audience is already convinced and is simply trying to understand the implications. But when the audience is skeptical, resistant, even unreceptive, one lets the listener discover the implicit change message so that it becomes the audience's own idea, and meaningful to them. |
| The listeners should be encouraged to identify with the protagonist | Much of the persuasive power of a springboard story derives from the fact that the audience identifies with the protagonist in such a way as to enable them to see things from another perspective. |

| | |
|---|---|
| The story should deal with a specific individual or organization | People are more likely to project onto single individuals than onto multiple individuals or groups. Specific individuals work better than anonymous groups or collections of organizations. |
| The protagonist should be prototypical of the organization's main business | The individual should be a central figure in the business of the organization. If the principal business is sales, it should be a salesman. If it is manufacturing, it should be someone in manufacturing. If it is a service organization with multidisciplinary teams, it should be the leader of such a team. |
| Other things being equal, true is better than invented | Our confidence in the veracity of a supposedly true story is usually not on very solid ground. But the apparent superiority of a true story over a wholly invented story in terms of communication is palpable. A true story with extrapolations into the future can work well even with difficult audiences. |
| Test, test, test | Only experience with an actual audience can tell us whether a story is going to work with that audience or not. A story can be tested on individuals or small groups before being tried out on a large group in a high-risk setting. |

# APPENDIX 2

# Some Elements for Using Visual Aids in Storytelling

**Some elements for using visual aids in storytelling**

| *Characteristic* | *Explanation* |
| --- | --- |
| Use visual aids to reinforce the storyteller's message | Overheads and slides can reinforce a presenter's message or hinder it. The richness or emptiness of the presenter's mental processes is laid bare in the visual aids that the presenter chooses to use. Visual aids serve as a lens for the presentation. If one has nothing to say, the visual aids will reveal this all too clearly. If one has something to communicate, the slides may help to focus the attention of the audience. If one's main point is a tangle of analytical abstractions, the visual aids will make this apparent. If one's communication is built on and around a springboard story, the visual aids can help emphasize that and strengthen it. |
| Use slides to keep the presentation on track | Visual aids can help you remember what you intended to say. Often the speaker loses the thread of his thought and can't recall where he is in the grand scheme of things, and so wanders on, flustered and lost. The audience knows that the presenter is lost. But there is nothing to be done. The presenter cannot tell the audience |

|  | that he is lost. Visual aids can serve as a navigational aid to get back on track. |
|---|---|
| Movement | Movement is the fuel of communication. Living things are in perpetual movement. Static aspects are likely to remind the audience—albeit subliminally—of death and dying. In a presentation, two things can move. One is you, the presenter. The other is the visual presentation—overheads or slide show—that you may use to accentuate what you have to say. One of the uses of visual aids is to create movement. In making a presentation, you can enact the story being told. |
| Use body movements to reinforce the message | Externally, you may not be moving, but rather standing still at the podium, but this does not imply passiveness and inaction. You may stir without motion. Physical immobility can reflect inner intensity. Use the tools at your disposal— voice, gestures, slides—to move, either visibly or inwardly. |
| Every movement in a slide show should have a purpose | There should be no movement, no effort in any direction, without some objective, without one's feeling inwardly a justification for them. Beware of random haphazard action that can distract the audience. Everything that happens in the presentation must have a definite purpose. It must be logical, coherent, natural, intuitive, and complete. |
| Don't despise visual aids | It is currently fashionable to criticize visual aids. And it is true that they can become the crutch of the lazy individual, someone who has nothing interesting to say, and imagines that a few visual aids will fuel the illusion that in reality there is something going on in the presenter's head. Nevertheless, when well designed, visual aids can make a major contribution to storytelling and communication. |

# APPENDIX 3

# Elements for Performing the Springboard Story

## Some elements for performing a springboard story[1]

| Characteristic | Explanation |
|---|---|
| Voice | The accent of the presenter is a pointing finger, singling out the key word, the high point of the text. It is a key dimension of the presentation, as it produces depth. There are many planes of speech that create perspective in a phrase. The most important word stands out most vividly defined in the very foreground of the sound plane. Less important words, less crisply delineated, create a series of deeper planes. It is not so much the volume as the quality of the accent. Accent can be combined with intonation, which may be caressing, ironical, scornful, respectful, and with rhythm. Pauses can highlight a word more loudly than a wild shout. |
| Understanding the audience | As the instigator of change, you should know what people are talking about at water coolers and boardrooms. You should understand the dynamics of the managers and how they are |

---

[1] Konstantin Stanislavsky, *An Actor's Handbook; An Alphabetical Arrangement of Concise Statements on Aspects of Acting*. (Edited and translated by Elizabeth Reynolds Hapgood. New York, Theatre Arts Books, 1963. Reprint, Methuen London, 1990.)

perceived. You should understand the level of
trust in the organization. You should be aware
of the latest rumors and gossip. You sense, dissect, weigh, discover, examine, study, analyze,
and intuit. You seek out everything relevant to
the enterprise, not simply the facts, but the
meaning of what you see and hear and feel.
While you are gathering this knowledge, you
will not know how it will be used, or what
import it will have. This is the material that will
feed the imagination, feelings, thoughts, and
will. You need it, however, in order to grasp the
values in the lives of the people you will speak
to. You implicitly reflect the inner cravings of
your audience. This will give authenticity to
what you say, regardless of content.

| | |
|---|---|
| Eyes | Nothing can be more awful or boring to watch than a presenter with vacant eyes. This is evidence that the presenter's soul is dormant. If the presenter's soul is dormant, no spark or fire is apt to light the listeners' minds. The vacant eye is the mirror of an empty soul. |
| Ownership | Take hold of the presentation as though it is your own. When you sense a real kinship with the presentation, you *become* the presentation. You must feel the story as though it is your very own flesh undergoing it. There must be nothing foreign or exotic. It is necessary that the audience feel your inner relationship to what you are saying. If it is not your own, if you have not made it your own, the audience will know it at once and you are lost. |
| Conviction | Truth in performance is not simply the factual accuracy of what you are saying, not some small contingent truth. It is what you, the presenter, genuinely believe. Even a true statement may become an untruth in the listener's mind if it is |

expressed hesitantly, whereas a flimsy hypothesis can be irresistibly convincing if expressed with conviction. If you begin to doubt even for a second the veracity of what you are saying, the audience will instantly pick this up, and the prospects for communication are lost. It will amount merely to going through motions, pretense, falseness, or public relations.

| | |
|---|---|
| Readiness | The writer may create when he is in the mood to communicate and when he gets the inspiration. As the presenter, you must be master of your inspiration and must know how to call it forth at the hour announced for the time of your presentation. |
| Practice, practice, practice | Amateurs fail to practice out of laziness or stupidity. It is the genuine professional who never stops trying to make the good even better. There is a tendency for even the professional to become neglectful of the necessity to practice and negligent in his habits. |
| Practice with an audience | To talk without an audience is the same as singing in a room without any resonance. To talk before an audience is like singing in a hall with excellent acoustics. The audience provides a sounding board, returning to the presenter live human emotions. The audience is a creative participant in the presentation. |
| Keeping one's edge | A presenter's creative mood will be unstable at first until the presentation is well rounded out. Again, later, when it gets worn, it will lose its keenness. Over time, you will know instinctively when there has been an unwanted discrepancy, and will find the mistake and correct it. All the time, you will continue to make the presentation while observing yourself. |

| Living the presentation | As a presenter, you are under the obligation to live your part inwardly, and then to give this experience an external embodiment in a clear articulate form. As a presenter, you must above all believe in your presentation. Truth cannot be separated from belief, nor belief from truth. And without both of them, it is impossible to stir your listeners, or to create anything. Believe in what you yourself say in your presentation, and you will be convincing. |

# APPENDIX 4

# Building up the Springboard Story: Four Different Structures

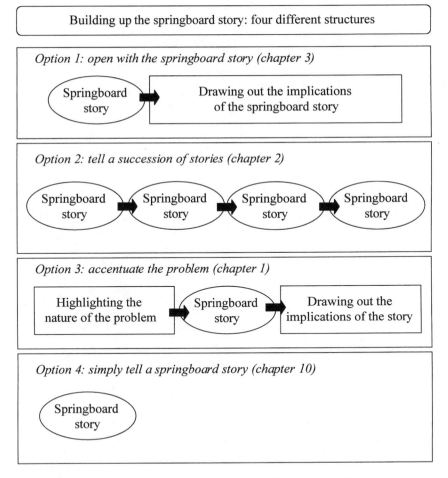

Building up the springboard story: four different structures

*Option 1: open with the springboard story (chapter 3)*

Springboard story → Drawing out the implications of the springboard story

*Option 2: tell a succession of stories (chapter 2)*

Springboard story → Springboard story → Springboard story → Springboard story

*Option 3: accentuate the problem (chapter 1)*

Highlighting the nature of the problem → Springboard story → Drawing out the implications of the story

*Option 4: simply tell a springboard story (chapter 10)*

Springboard story

*A discussion of the four structures may be found in chapter 10.*

# APPENDIX 5

# Examples of Springboard Stories

## Examples of springboard stories: Zambia and the CDC

What will the twenty-first century be like? What I want to suggest to you is that the future is going to be very much like today.

Thus, in June, 1995, a health worker in Kamana, Zambia, logged on to the Center for Disease Control web-site and got the answer to a question on how to treat malaria.

This story happened, not in June 2015, but in June 1995. This is not a rich country: it is Zambia, one of the least developed countries in the world. It is not even the capital of the country: it is six hundred kilometers away. But the most striking aspect of the picture is this: our organization isn't in it. Our organization doesn't have its know-how and expertise organized in such a way that someone like the health worker in Zambia can have access to it.

But just imagine if it had! We could get ourselves organized so that professionals have access to the resources needed, just in time and just enough.

Thus when it comes to best practice - our teams will want not every best practice under the sun, but just the lessons of experience that are relevant to the particular task in hand. Similarly with the bibliography: our teams will want not the whole Library of Congress, just the references and citations that are relevant to the particular project. With policies and guidelines, our teams don't need the whole massive operational manual and all the other policy guidelines that have accumulated over decades - just the sections that are relevant to the job under way. Again, with country information, our teams don't want everything we know about the countries, just the people and correspondence that lead up to the work now ongoing - in effect, "the story so far." Also, they don't want all the previous reports - just the reports that had been done in the same field as the task at hand. And in signaling who knows what, the team wants to know not who are the gurus generally, but rather who can answer questions on key issues relevant to the particular area of work. Equally, in analytical tools, the team wants spreadsheets showing previous economic, financial and technical analyses of earlier work in the same area, not everything that has been done.

And if we can put all these elements in place for the task teams, why not for the clients? They have exactly the same needs as the employees. Imagine: if we can do this, true partnership can emerge. Moreover, a whole group of stakeholders around the world who currently lack access to the intellectual resources of the organization will suddenly be in the picture. It will enable a different relationship with a wider group of clients and partners and stakeholders around the world. It adds up to a new organizational strategy.

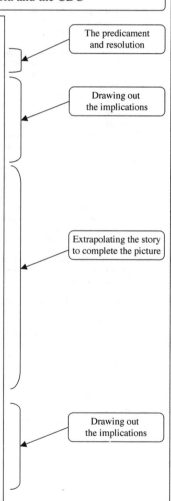

The predicament and resolution

Drawing out the implications

Extrapolating the story to complete the picture

Drawing out the implications

## Examples of springboard stories: Chile

A leader of one of the multi-disciplinary task teams was in Santiago, Chile, when our client contacted her and asked: quick, what is the experience of your organization in other countries in dealing with the demands of school teachers?

As it happened, she didn't have the full answer to the question on hand.

So she contacted the advisory service of the education network who was able to assemble for her experiences from other staff working in other countries around the world that were analogous to the situation of Chile.

The material was sent to Santiago electronically and the task team leader was able synthesize the material and in a matter of hours, the client had the answer - a feat that would have been impossible without having the advisory service make the connections between the task team leader and the other staff working on similar issues in other countries. The client was delighted with the responsiveness, and the transaction led to an intensified collaboration in the sector.

What will happen in the future? What we have learnt from the Chile experience is now recognized as being valuable. The material can be edited for further re-use and entered into the knowledge base, so that when a new client with similar problems, say, a country in Africa, asks another task team for the global experience in this area, the answer is readily accessible through the organization's Intranet.

This will only happen if three conditions are in place: first, if there is a classification system that enables one to find the Chile synthesis in a large knowledge base; secondly, if the education advisory service has an easy-to-contact human being who can answer questions and guide the search; and thirdly, if there is institutional technology platform that makes it easy to find things across organizational boundaries.

So as the story continues, the African experience will be edited for further re-use, and entered into the knowledge base. Other inputs from other parts of the organization - and outside - can also be added.

Later on, when the system is fully developed, and the expertise is made available externally, when yet another client - say from Asia - has a question in the same area, there are new possibilities. The client can go into the knowledge base on its own through the World Wide Web, and find the Chile synthesis, find the African synthesis, find the other inputs, and then either use them on their own, or ask for assistance in applying it to its local situation. In this way, the know-how is made available quickly, inexpensively, for all the world to use.

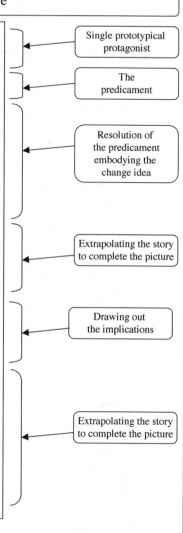

Single prototypical protagonist

The predicament

Resolution of the predicament embodying the change idea

Extrapolating the story to complete the picture

Drawing out the implications

Extrapolating the story to complete the picture

## Examples of springboard stories: Yemen

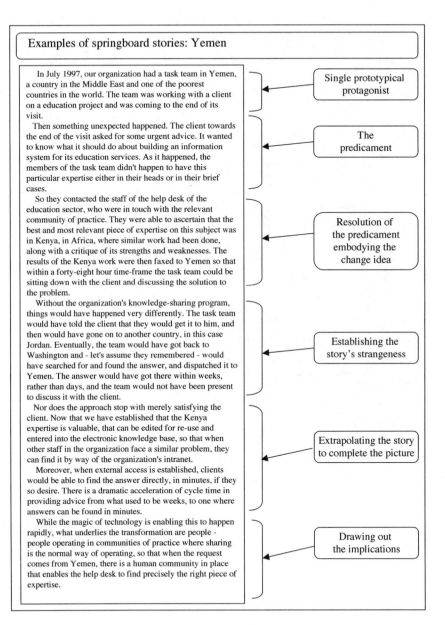

In July 1997, our organization had a task team in Yemen, a country in the Middle East and one of the poorest countries in the world. The team was working with a client on a education project and was coming to the end of its visit.

**Single prototypical protagonist**

Then something unexpected happened. The client towards the end of the visit asked for some urgent advice. It wanted to know what it should do about building an information system for its education services. As it happened, the members of the task team didn't happen to have this particular expertise either in their heads or in their brief cases.

**The predicament**

So they contacted the staff of the help desk of the education sector, who were in touch with the relevant community of practice. They were able to ascertain that the best and most relevant piece of expertise on this subject was in Kenya, in Africa, where similar work had been done, along with a critique of its strengths and weaknesses. The results of the Kenya work were then faxed to Yemen so that within a forty-eight hour time-frame the task team could be sitting down with the client and discussing the solution to the problem.

**Resolution of the predicament embodying the change idea**

Without the organization's knowledge-sharing program, things would have happened very differently. The task team would have told the client that they would get it to him, and then would have gone on to another country, in this case Jordan. Eventually, the team would have got back to Washington and - let's assume they remembered - would have searched for and found the answer, and dispatched it to Yemen. The answer would have got there within weeks, rather than days, and the team would not have been present to discuss it with the client.

**Establishing the story's strangeness**

Nor does the approach stop with merely satisfying the client. Now that we have established that the Kenya expertise is valuable, that can be edited for re-use and entered into the electronic knowledge base, so that when other staff in the organization face a similar problem, they can find it by way of the organization's intranet.

Moreover, when external access is established, clients would be able to find the answer directly, in minutes, if they so desire. There is a dramatic acceleration of cycle time in providing advice from what used to be weeks, to one where answers can be found in minutes.

**Extrapolating the story to complete the picture**

While the magic of technology is enabling this to happen rapidly, what underlies the transformation are people - people operating in communities of practice where sharing is the normal way of operating, so that when the request comes from Yemen, there is a human community in place that enables the help desk to find precisely the right piece of expertise.

**Drawing out the implications**

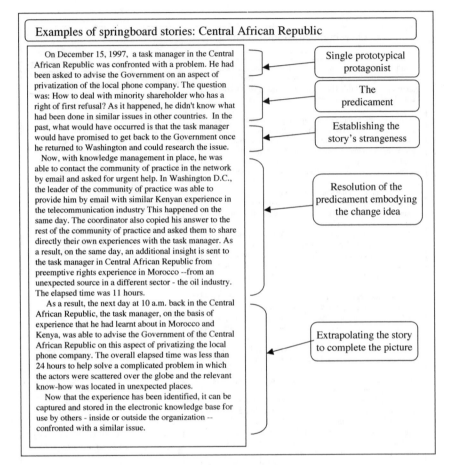

Examples of springboard stories: Central African Republic

On December 15, 1997, a task manager in the Central African Republic was confronted with a problem. He had been asked to advise the Government on an aspect of privatization of the local phone company. The question was: How to deal with minority shareholder who has a right of first refusal? As it happened, he didn't know what had been done in similar issues in other countries. In the past, what would have occurred is that the task manager would have promised to get back to the Government once he returned to Washington and could research the issue.

Now, with knowledge management in place, he was able to contact the community of practice in the network by email and asked for urgent help. In Washington D.C., the leader of the community of practice was able to provide him by email with similar Kenyan experience in the telecommunication industry This happened on the same day. The coordinator also copied his answer to the rest of the community of practice and asked them to share directly their own experiences with the task manager. As a result, on the same day, an additional insight is sent to the task manager in Central African Republic from preemptive rights experience in Morocco --from an unexpected source in a different sector - the oil industry. The elapsed time was 11 hours.

As a result, the next day at 10 a.m. back in the Central African Republic, the task manager, on the basis of experience that he had learnt about in Morocco and Kenya, was able to advise the Government of the Central African Republic on this aspect of privatizing the local phone company. The overall elapsed time was less than 24 hours to help solve a complicated problem in which the actors were scattered over the globe and the relevant know-how was located in unexpected places.

Now that the experience has been identified, it can be captured and stored in the electronic knowledge base for use by others - inside or outside the organization -- confronted with a similar issue.

Single prototypical protagonist

The predicament

Establishing the story's strangeness

Resolution of the predicament embodying the change idea

Extrapolating the story to complete the picture

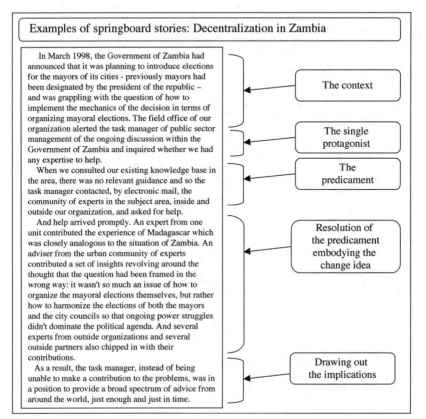

Examples of springboard stories: Decentralization in Zambia

In March 1998, the Government of Zambia had announced that it was planning to introduce elections for the mayors of its cities - previously mayors had been designated by the president of the republic – and was grappling with the question of how to implement the mechanics of the decision in terms of organizing mayoral elections. The field office of our organization alerted the task manager of public sector management of the ongoing discussion within the Government of Zambia and inquired whether we had any expertise to help.

When we consulted our existing knowledge base in the area, there was no relevant guidance and so the task manager contacted, by electronic mail, the community of experts in the subject area, inside and outside our organization, and asked for help.

And help arrived promptly. An expert from one unit contributed the experience of Madagascar which was closely analogous to the situation of Zambia. An adviser from the urban community of experts contributed a set of insights revolving around the thought that the question had been framed in the wrong way: it wasn't so much an issue of how to organize the mayoral elections themselves, but rather how to harmonize the elections of both the mayors and the city councils so that ongoing power struggles didn't dominate the political agenda. And several experts from outside organizations and several outside partners also chipped in with their contributions.

As a result, the task manager, instead of being unable to make a contribution to the problems, was in a position to provide a broad spectrum of advice from around the world, just enough and just in time.

The context

The single protagonist

The predicament

Resolution of the predicament embodying the change idea

Drawing out the implications

## Examples of springboard stories: 6. Pakistan highways

In August, 1998, the government of Pakistan asked our field office in Pakistan for help in the highway sector. They were experiencing widespread pavement failure. The highways were falling apart. They wanted to try a different technology, a technology that we have not supported or recommended in the past. And they wanted our advice within a few days.

I think it's fair to say that in the past we would not have been able to respond to this kind of question within this time frame. We would have either said we couldn't help, or have said to them that this technology is not one that we recommend or we might have proposed to send a team to Pakistan. The team would look around, write a report, review the report, redraft the report, send the report to the government, and eventually, perhaps three, six, nine months later, provide a response. But by then it's too late. By then things have moved on in Pakistan.

What actually happened was something quite different. The task team leader in our field office in Pakistan sent an email and contacted the community of highway experts inside and outside our organization (a community that has been put together over time) and asked for help within forty-eight hours. And he got it. The same day the task manager in the highway sector in Jordan replied that, as it happened, Jordan was using this technology with very promising results. The same day a highway expert in our Argentina office replied and said that he was writing a book on the subject and was able to give the genealogy of the technology over several decades and continents. And shortly after that, the head of the highways authority in South Africa – an outside partner who is part of the community - chipped in with South Africa's experience over several decades with something like the same technology. And New Zealand provided some guidelines that it had developed for the use of the technology. And so the task manager in Pakistan was able to go back to the Pakistan government and say: this is the best that we as an organization can put together on this subject, and then the dialogue can start as to how to adapt that experience elsewhere to Pakistan's situation.

And now that we have realized that we as an organization know something about a subject we didn't realize we knew anything about, now we can incorporate what we have learnt in our knowledge base so that any staff in the organization anywhere at any time can tap into it. And the vision is that we can make this available externally through the World Wide Web, so that anyone in the world will be able to log on and get answers to questions like this on which we have some know-how, as well as on any of the other myriad subjects on which we have managed to assemble some expertise.

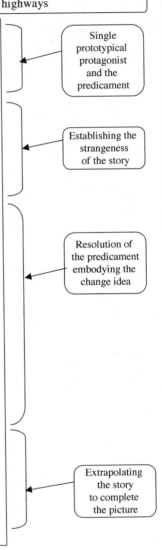

Single prototypical protagonist and the predicament

Establishing the strangeness of the story

Resolution of the predicament embodying the change idea

Extrapolating the story to complete the picture

# APPENDIX 6

# Knowledge Management Chart

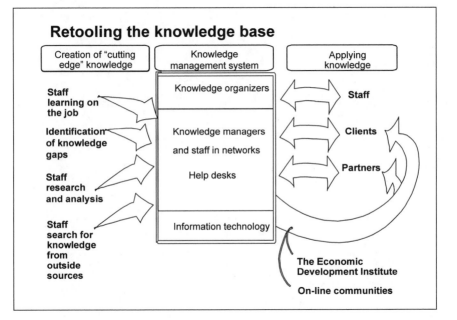

# Bibliography

Abram, David. *The Spell of the Sensuous: Perception and Language in a More-than-Human World.* New York: Pantheon Books, 1997.

Amidon, Debra M. *Innovation Strategy for the Knowledge Economy: The Ken Awakening.* Boston: Butterworth-Heinemann, 1997.

Aristotle. *The Art of Rhetoric,* translated by H.C. Lawson-Tancred. London: Penguin Books, 1991.

Baudrillard, Jean. *Seduction,* translated by Brian Singer. New York: St. Martin's Press, 1990.

Bettelheim, Bruno. *The Uses of Enchantment: The Meaning and Importance of Fairy Tales.* New York: Knopf, 1976.

Birkerts, Sven. *The Gutenberg Elegies: The Fate of Reading in an Electronic Age.* Boston: Faber and Faber, 1994.

Bohm, David. *On Dialogue,* edited by Lee Nichol. London, New York: Routledge, 1996.

Brooks, Peter. *Reading for the Plot: Design and Intention in Narrative.* New York: A.A. Knopf, 1984.

Brunner, Jerome. "Culture and Human Development: A New Look," *Human Development,* Vol. 33, 1990, pp. 344–355.

Calvino, Italo. *Six Memos for the Next Millennium,* translated by Patrick Creagh. London: Vintage, 1996.

Capra, Fritjof. *The Web of Life: A New Scientific Understanding of Living Systems.* New York: Anchor Books, 1996.

Carse, James P. *Finite and Infinite Games.* New York: Free Press, 1986.

Davenport, Thomas H., and Laurence Prusak. *Working Knowledge: How Organizations Manage What They Know.* Boston: Harvard Business School Press, 1997.

Deming, W. Edwards. *Out of the Crisis*. Cambridge, MA: Massachusetts Institute of Technology, Center for Advanced Engineering Study, 1986.

Denning, Stephen. "The Seven Basics of Knowledge Management." *Communication Technology Decisions*. London: World Trade Group Ltd., Issue One, Winter 1999/00.

Denning, Stephen, et al. *What Is Knowledge Management?* Washington, DC: World Bank, 1998.

Franck, Frederick. *The Zen of Seeing; Seeing/Drawing as Meditation*. New York: Vintage Books, 1973.

Gabriel, Yannis. *Storytelling in Organizations: Facts, Fictions, and Fantasies.* Oxford: Oxford University Press, 2000.

Grudin, Robert. *On Dialogue: An Essay in Free Thought*. Boston: Houghton Mifflin, 1996.

Henri, Robert. *The Art Spirit*. Philadelphia and London: J. B. Lippincott Company, 1923. Reprint, New York: Harper & Row, 1984.

Herrigel, Eugen. *Zen in the Art of Archery*, translated by R.F.C. Hull. New York: Pantheon Books, 1953. Reprint, New York: Vintage Books, 1989.

Hirshfield, Jane. *Nine Gates: Entering the Mind of Poetry*. New York: HarperCollins, 1997.

Holtshouse, D., and R. Ruggles (Editors), Christopher Meyer. *The Knowledge Advantage: 14 Visionaries Define Marketplace Success in the New Economy*. New Hampshire: Capstone, 1999.

Jakobson, R. "Linguistics and Poetry" in *Style and Language,* edited by T. A. Sebeok. Cambridge, MA: MIT Press, pp. 350–377.

Kosko, Bart. *Fuzzy Thinking: The New Science of Fuzzy Logic*. New York: Hyperion, 1993.

Kotter, J. *Leading Change*. Boston: Harvard Business School Press, 1996.

Mandler, George. *Mind and Body: Psychology of Emotion and Stress*. New York: W.W. Norton, 1984.

Monmonier, Mark S. *How to Lie with Maps*. Chicago: University of Chicago Press, 1991.

Nonaka, Ikujiro, and Hirotaka Takeuchi. *The Knowledge-Creating Company: How Japanese Companies Create the Dynamics of Innovation.* New York: Oxford University Press, 1995.

O'Dell, Carla S., and C. Jackson Grayson with Nilly Essaides. *If Only We Knew What We Know: The Transfer of Internal Knowledge and Best Practice.* New York: Free Press, 1998.

Pirsig, Robert B. *Zen and the Art of Motorcycle Maintenance: An Inquiry into Values.* New York: Morrow, 1974.

Plato. *Phaedrus and the Seventh and Eighth Letters.* Translated by Walter Hamilton. Harmondsworth: Penguin, 1973.

Plato. *The Republic* (Penguin Classics), translated by Desmond Lee. Viking Press, 1979.

Polkinghorne, Donald E. *Narrative Knowing and the Human Sciences.* Albany, NY: State University of New York Press, 1988.

Schwartz, Howard S., *Narcissistic Process and Corporate Decay: The Theory of the Organizational Ideal.* New York: New York University Press, 1990.

Stanislavsky, Konstantin. *An Actor's Handbook; An Alphabetical Arrangement of Concise Statements on Aspects of Acting,* edited and translated by Elizabeth Reynolds Hapgood. New York: Theatre Arts Books, 1963. Reprint, Methuen London, 1990.

Stewart, Ian. *Does God Play Dice?: The Mathematics of Chaos.* Oxford, New York: B. Blackwell, 1989.

Stone, R. *The Healing Art of Storytelling: A Sacred Journey of Personal Discovery.* New York: Hyperion, 1996.

Suzuki, Shunryu. *Zen Mind, Beginner's Mind,* edited by Trudy Dixon. New York: Walker/Weatherhill, 1970.

Tufte, Edward R. *The Visual Display of Quantitative Information.* Cheshire, CT: Graphics Press, 1983.

Weick, Karl E. *Sensemaking in Organizations.* Thousand Oaks, CA: Sage Publications, 1995.

Weick, Karl E., and Larry D. Browning. "Argument and Narration in Organizational Communication," *Yearly Review of Management of the*

*Journal of Management,* edited by J. G. Hund and J. D. Blair, Vol. 12, No. 2, pp. 243–259 (1986).

Wheatley, Margaret, and Myron Kellner-Rogers. *A Simpler Way.* San Francisco: Berrett-Koehler Publishers, 1996.

# Acknowledgments

In a book in which the characters have been anonymous, it may seem strange to start naming names at this stage. My stylistic predecessor, Professor Eugen Herrigel, in his little book *Zen in the Art of Archery*, pursued the anonymity of his actors through to the conclusion. Yet, obviously this book could never have emerged without hundreds of people in countries around the world who have helped—in various ways—to prod, stimulate, encourage, and inspire me. I am particularly grateful to Debra Amidon, Peter Armstrong, Elliot Berg, Keith Bradley, Alison Brandt, Bob Buckman, Elias Carayannis, Roberto Chavez, Don Cohen, Janet Coleman, Louis Currat, Tom Davenport, David De Ferranti, Stephanie Denning, Lyn Dowling, Amer Zafar Durrani, Carole Evangelista, Asif Faiz, Nicolas Gorjestani, David Gray, Jack Grayson, Kent Greenes, Margaret Grieco, Adnan Hassan, Robert Hiebeler, Hollis Heimbouch, Ian Heggie, Dan Holtshouse, Steen Jorgensen, Seth Weaver Kahan, Omer Karasapan, Phil Karp, Arti Kirch, Michael Klein, Bruno Laporte, Dorothy Leonard, Kent Lineback, Ted Lumley, Graciela Luna, Peter Midgley, Ikujiro Nonaka, Carla O'Dell, Martha Pattillo-Siv, Michel Pommier, Larry Prusak, Jean-François Rischard, Rudy Ruggles, Melissie Rumizen, Charles Savage, Ismaïl Serageldin, Mary Lou Simmermacher, Lesley Shneier, Kathy Sierra, David Skyrme, Jimmy Neil Smith, David Skyrme, Tom Stewart, Richard Stone, Paul Strebel, Phil Sutherland, Tache, Anuradha Vittachi, Etienne Wenger, Steven Wilson, Douglas Weidner, Jan Wyllie, Jim Wolfensohn, and Shengman Zhang, along with all the many people I have met through the American Productivity and Quality Center, Business Intelligence (U.K.), the Ernst & Young Center for Innovation, the Storytelling Foundation International, World Trade Group, and the World Bank Group. Above all, I want to thank my audiences from whom I learned so much.

# About the Author

Stephen Denning was born in Sydney, Australia. He studied psychology and law at the University of Sydney (Australia) and law at the Oxford University (U.K.). He has held many positions in the World Bank where he is program director of knowledge management. He contributes to knowledge management and organizational learning publications and presents frequently at leading professional management conferences.

He has published a novel *The Painter: A Novel of Pursuit* (iUniverse: 2000), and a collection of poems: *Sonnets 2000* (iUniverse: 2000).

His website may be found at www.stevedenning.com

He lives in Washington, D.C. with his wife and daughter.

# About
# KMCI Press
*Powerful Knowledge for*
*Knowledge Professionals*

KMCI Press is an exciting publishing partnership that unites the Knowledge Management Consortium International (KMCI), the leading organization for knowledge management professionals, and Butterworth–Heinemann's Business group and Digital Press imprints, one of the premier publishers of knowledge management books.

KMCI Press publishes authoritative and innovative books that educate, unify, and empower all knowledge management communities, from students and beginning professionals to chief knowledge officers. KMCI Press books present definitive and leading-edge ideas of the KMCI itself, establish industry standards, and bring clarity and authoritative information to a dynamic and emerging profession. \

KMCI Press books explore the opportunities, demands, and benefits knowledge management brings to organizations and defines important and emerging knowledge management disciplines and topics, including:

- Professional roles, functions, and certification standards
- Vertical industry best practices and applications
- Technologies, including knowledge portals and data and document management
- Strategies, methodologies, and decision-making frameworks

The Knowledge Management Consortium International (KMCI) is the only major member organization specifically for knowledge management professionals, with thousands of worldwide members including individuals in the professional and academic fields as well as leading companies, institutions, and other organizations concerned with knowledge management, organizational change, and intellectual capital.